Labor and
Economic Growth
in Five Asian Countries

Labor and Economic Growth in Five Asian Countries

SOUTH KOREA, MALAYSIA,
TAIWAN, THAILAND,
AND THE PHILIPPINES

WALTER GALENSON

New York
Westport, Connecticut
London

Library of Congress Cataloging-in-Publication Data

Galenson, Walter, 1914–
    Labor and economic growth in five Asian countries : South Korea,
Malaysia, Taiwan, Thailand, and the Philippines / Walter Galenson.
      p. cm.
    Includes bibliographical references and index.
    ISBN 0–275–94200–7 (alk. paper)
    1. Labor market—Asia.   2. Asia—Economic conditions—1945–
I. Title.
    HD5811.85.A6G35   1992
    331.12′095—dc20   91–33883

British Library Cataloguing in Publication Data is available.

Library of Congress Catalog Card Number: 91–33883
ISBN: 0–275–94200–7

First published in 1992

Praeger Publishers, One Madison Avenue, New York, NY 10010
An imprint of Greenwood Publishing Group, Inc.

Printed in the United States of America

The paper used in this book complies with the Permanent
Paper Standard issued by the National Information Standards
Organization (Z39.48–1984).

10 9 8 7 6 5 4 3 2 1

*For
Joel
and
Joshua*

Contents

Tables

Labor and
Economic Growth
in Five Asian Countries

1

Introduction

The relationships between economic development and the operation and structure of labor markets have not been explored thoroughly. In part this is due to problems of measurement, but there are also difficulties stemming from the heterogeneity of the forces that affect the labor market. For example, the political background and social characteristics of a country have an important influence on the manner in which its people work, and this in turn affects productivity. It is easier to analyze such factors as investment rates and foreign trade because they are readily quantifiable and can lead to clear-cut conclusions.

This does not mean that there is a complete vacuum in our knowledge of the contribution of particular aspects of the labor market to development, or of the impact of development on the labor market. For example, certain labor-force regularities appear to hold under widely varying conditions. As development proceeds, the proportion of the labor force in the industrial sector increases at the expense of agriculture, only in turn to yield to the service sector. Wages may start out at the subsistence level in what

Arthur Lewis called the state of an unlimited supply of labor, but they increase inevitably as development proceeds. Hours of work tend to decline as workers are able to afford to substitute leisure for income.

Nevertheless, even these relationships are by no means uniform across countries and over time. Agricultural employment may continue to provide a substantial share of total employment where farm exports constitute an important engine of growth. Wages can rise more or less rapidly depending on a number of factors, including government policy. Long hours of work may continue to prevail where cultural factors favor a preference for income over leisure.

It is the purpose of this study to examine how the labor market changes as development proceeds. The labor market is defined broadly to include not only wages and hours, but also such additional conditions of employment as fringe benefits, safety and health measures, and pensions. It is also comprised of such structural features as trade unions, employer associations, and collective bargaining relationships. The characteristics of the labor force—age, skill, sex, levels of education—are part of the picture. Not least in importance is government policy as manifested by legislation and administration.

What has become standard procedure would dictate the development of an econometric model through which the effect of each labor attribute on growth could be estimated. Unfortunately, neither the available data nor the nature of many of the relevant variables lend themselves to an exercise of this kind. For example, it might be possible to assign ordinal values to government attitudes toward trade unions. However, not only do these change over time, sometimes quite rapidly as one administration succeeds another, but it is likely that different observers would not agree on the ordering. This is a problem that bedevils the determination of even narrower labor matters such as comparable worth in the differentiation of wages, where widely varying results may flow from alternative job evaluation systems.

Even where relevant data are quantitative in form, their interpretation may be difficult. For example, an industrial relations system that contributes to uninterrupted work might be regarded as superior to one that results in frequent work stoppages, which can be measured by available strike statistics. But this reading is by no means unambiguous; the absence of strikes may simply signal a cowed labor force that is not highly motivated and less productive than one which has more freedom to express grievances.

Tracking labor-market changes that flow from economic development rather than determine it, is less difficult because cause and effect relationships tend to be easier to disentangle. Even here, however, there are problems, since economic growth is not the only influence at work. Changes in income distribution, for example, can be determined more by the political climate than by changes in the economy.

All of this said, the purpose of this study is to compare the experiences of five Asian countries in an effort to distill out any regularities in the pattern of labor market behavior during the transition from primary reliance on agriculture to some level of industrialization. The five nations in the sample, together with their populations in 1988 (in millions), are as follows:

South Korea	42
Malaysia	17
Philippines	60
Taiwan	20
Thailand	54

The choice of countries was based on several factors. They are all Asian and middle sized. The problems faced by the Asian giants— China, India, Pakistan, Bangladesh, Indonesia—are of another order of magnitude. It would have been desirable to include Sri Lanka, but the civil war that has been raging there for the past decade puts it in a different category. The same is true of Burma, which has been in self-imposed isolation, and the war-ravaged countries of Indochina. Hong Kong and Singapore are city-states with truncated economies.

A second factor in sample selection was that all the countries chosen have experienced economic growth, though at considerably different rates. The Philippines are marginal in this respect, but their inclusion is useful for comparative purposes.

Finally, there is the question of cultural homogeneity. There is a strong Chinese influence in South Korea and Taiwan, somewhat less in Malaysia. Thailand and the Philippines have different backgrounds, but have more in common with their Asian neighbors than with developing countries in Africa or Latin America. None of these five countries can be characterized as pure democracies, but on the other hand their governments have not been totalitarian. During the past 40 years they have experienced periods of military rule, but all have tended to move in the direction of more representative forms of government. This is very important for labor market institutions.

THE RECORD OF ECONOMIC GROWTH

Data on the average annual growth of the gross domestic product for the five countries in our sample for the periods 1965–1980 and 1980–1988 are shown in Table 1.1. Annual data for individual years between 1979 and 1988 appear in Table 1.2. It is clear that South Korea and Taiwan are in a class by themselves, and not only with respect to the Asian countries. If we take the period 1980–1988, for example, the lower middle-income developing countries of the world increased their Gross Domestic Product (GDP) by 2.6

Table 1.1
Average Annual Growth of the Gross Domestic Product, 1965–1988 (percent)

	1965-1980	1980-1988
South Korea	9.5	9.9
Malaysia	7.3	4.6
Philippines	5.9	0.1
Taiwan	9.7	8.1
Thailand	7.2	6.0

Sources: World Bank, *World Development Report* (Washington, 1990); Republic of China, *Taiwan Statistical Data Book* (Taipei, 1990).

Table 1.2
Average Annual Growth of the Gross Domestic Product, 1979–1989
(percent)

	South Korea	Malaysia	Philippines	Taiwan	Thailand
1979	7.5	9.5	6.3	8.2	5.0
1980	-3.3	7.5	5.3	7.3	4.7
1981	6.9	6.9	3.8	6.2	6.3
1982	7.4	6.0	2.9	3.6	4.0
1983	12.1	6.4	1.1	8.5	7.2
1984	9.6	7.9	-6.3	10.6	7.1
1985	6.9	-1.1	-4.5	5.0	3.6
1986	12.6	1.3	1.4	11.6	4.4
1987	11.9	5.3	4.9	12.3	8.1
1988	11.3	8.9	6.5	7.3	10.9
1989	6.5	8.5	5.8	7.3	11.0

Sources: World Bank, *World Tables* (Washington, 1989–1990); Republic of China, *Statistical Yearbook* (Taipei, 1989), Table 47.

percent annually, and the upper middle-income group by 3.3 percent. Malaysia and Thailand did not do as well as South Korea and Taiwan, but their growth was satisfactory by international standards. The Philippines did relatively well in the earlier period, but performed dismally in the 1980s.

Taiwan has been remarkable for its high and sustained rate of economic growth. Beginning with 1960, there were only four years in which its GDP annual growth rate fell below 6 percent. In 1974 and 1975, and again in 1982, the international oil crises led to recession in the industrial nations and hindered Taiwan's exports. The year 1984 started off well, but export volume fell in the latter half of the year and continued weak into 1985 due largely to a reduction of demand in the United States, Taiwan's principal customer.

South Korea has also had a remarkably high and steady rate of economic growth. It weathered the oil shock of the 1970s very well due to good economic management. A large increase in oil prices during 1979–1980, plus a failure of the rice crop, led to a severe recession, and for the first time since the Korean war the GDP actually fell. Growth soon resumed, however, reaching extremely high levels for the years 1986 to 1988.

Malaysia and Thailand might be called the growth twins of South Asia. Their average rates of annual GDP increases for the entire period since 1965 have been very close, but the year-to-year patterns differed. Malaysian growth averaged about 6 percent during the 1960s despite confrontation with Indonesia, separation from Singapore, and the Malay-Chinese riots. Growth rose substantially during the 1970s, and the 1980s started off well, only to be halted by a severe depression during 1985 and 1986 resulting from falling world prices for such key export commodities as petroleum, palm oil, rubber, and tin. Had it not been for these two bad years, Malaysia would have had a very respectable 6-percent growth rate during the 1980s.

Thailand also experienced rapid and sustained growth during the 1960s. The next decade was generally satisfactory apart from a slowdown in 1974 and 1975, with 1978 a banner year in which the GDP increased by 10.6 percent. There were several years of slower growth from 1980 to 1982 in reaction to the world recession, and again in 1985 and 1986, but subsequently a flood of foreign investment and sharply rising exports resulted in double-digit growth in 1988.

The Philippines stand out as the laggard in our group of countries. Actually, its economy did not do badly from 1965 to 1980, when it averaged almost 6 percent per annum, relative success among developing countries elsewhere. But the economic downturn of the early 1980s was very damaging to the Philippines, which slid into a full-fledged depression because of worsening terms of trade, a large accumulation of foreign debt that led to a stoppage of international credit, and the collapse of the manufacturing sector. As a result of these dismal years, the GDP in 1986 was about equal to that of 1980. Recovery set in during 1987 due mainly to sound economic management, but it is not yet clear that the country has achieved a sustainable growth path comparable to those of our other four countries.

Since all of these countries underwent substantial increases in population during the years under review, the GDP rates must be adjusted downward to transform them into GDP per capita. The results are shown in Table 1.3. The figure of 7.1 percent for Taiwan meant that by the end of the 1980s, despite its rapid population growth, Taiwan had raised itself out of the developing country category and had drawn even with Portugal. South Korea was in the same situation. Malaysia and Thailand could still be called developing countries by the end of the decade, but Malaysian per capita income exceeded that of countries like Costa Rica and Chile, while Thailand's income was higher than that of such Central American countries as El Salvador, Guatemala, and Honduras. A combination of rapid population growth and poor economic performance consigned the Philippines to the per capita income levels of Senegal, Zimbabwe, and Egypt.

In the constellation of developing countries, four of the nations in our sample stand out as among the most successful in the world during the last three decades. Their experience may help illuminate the path that other nations may follow in the coming years.

Table 1.3
Gross National Product per Capita, 1965–1988 (U.S. dollars)

	1988	Average annual rate of per capita growth, 1965–88 (percent)
South Korea	3600	6.8
Malaysia	1940	4.0
Philippines	630	1.6
Taiwan	6177	7.1[a]
Thailand	1000	4.0

Sources: World Bank, *World Development Report* (Washington, 1990); Republic of China, *Taiwan Statistical Data Book* (Taipei, 1988), Table 3–33; Republic of China, *Statistical Yearbook* (Taipei, 1989), Table 40.
[a]1965–1987

FACTORS CONTRIBUTING TO GROWTH

Particular government and private policies contribute to or detract from the possibilities of economic growth. Among them are the rate of investment, foreign trade, foreign assistance, and military expenditures. The countries under examination differ from one another with respect to these variables. A brief review of the differences may help set the stage for looking at labor markets.

A country that consumes all it produces can hardly expect to advance economically. Moreover, misplaced investment can impede growth by squandering scarce resources. Productive investment is needed as a condition for progress.

Table 1.4 contains investment data for the years 1965, 1980, and 1988. South Korea invested less out of its GDP than the other countries in 1965, but by 1987 its investment share was the highest in the group. Taiwan reached a peak in 1980 and then dropped back, while the Philippine rate was substantial until the onset of its 1980 depression.

There is some difference of opinion over the effectiveness of the sharp spurt of South Korean investment during the 1970s, mainly in heavy and chemical industries. A World Bank report concluded that as a result of the investment drive, "some of the production and export objectives were eventually realized, but its dominant

Table 1.4
Gross Domestic Investment as a Percentage of Gross Domestic Product, 1965, 1980, and 1988

	1965	1980	1988
South Korea	15	31	30
Malaysia	20	30	26
Philippines	21	31	17
Taiwan	23	34	20
Thailand	20	26	28

Sources: World Bank, *World Tables* (Washington, 1989–1990); Republic of China, *Statistical Yearbook* (Taipei, 1989), Table 42.

effects—underutilized capacity, 'crowding out' of traditional export industries, and a sharp decline in the incremental capital-output ratio—were unfortunately reminiscent of experiences elsewhere."[1] Other analysts maintained that "there is no hard evidence that Korea's investments were in fact poor. The judgment that the investment drive was a poor idea was made in 1980–1982, when excess capacity was large and the second oil shock hurt the chemical industry in particular. Today it is apparent that many of these industries have gained in export share. The automobile industry is a case in point."[2] This illustrates the problem of determining an effective investment policy. It is difficult to evaluate its merits *ex post* to say nothing of *ex ante*. In this case, South Korea's subsequent growth experience suggests that the investment was not misdirected.

The average investment ratios of the lower middle-income countries—a group that includes the Philippines, Malaysia, and Thailand by World Bank definition—were 19 percent in 1965 and 23 percent in 1988. They were 24 percent in both 1965 and 1986 for upper middle-income countries, where South Korea and Taiwan fall. It would be necessary to perform a year-to-year analysis to make more accurate comparisons, but the data do suggest that the investment ratio alone does not account for the superior growth pattern of the Asian countries. Indeed, a number of countries that are not known for having achieved high rates of economic growth—Algeria, Peru, Poland, and Yugoslavia, to name a few—invested heavily during some of these years.

There is general agreement among development economists that encouragement of foreign trade yields better results than substituting domestic production for imports by a policy of protectionism. This idea owes its theoretical origin to the famous Heckscher-Ohlin theorem, and it has considerable empirical support. The growth of exports and imports for the five Asian countries, together with the average rates for middle-income countries, are shown in Table 1.5. It appears from the data that South Korean trade expanded very rapidly, with Taiwan not far behind. Thailand came next, followed by Malaysia. The Philippine figures speak for them-

Table 1.5
Average Annual Growth of Exports and Imports, 1965–1988 (percent)

	Exports		Imports	
	1965-1980	1980-1988	1965-1980	1980-1988
South Korea	27.2	14.7	15.2	9.9
Malaysia	4.4	9.4	2.9	0.4
Philippines	4.7	0.4	2.9	-1.7
Taiwan	19.0	12.7	15.1	12.1
Thailand	8.5	11.3	4.1	6.2
Lower middle income developing countries	5.8	6.0	5.2	-0.2
Upper middle income developing countries	0.9	4.4	6.8	1.4

Sources: World Bank, *World Development Report* (Washington, 1990); Republic of China, *Statistical Yearbook* (Taipei, 1989), Table 209.

selves; Philippine trade did not even expand as rapidly as it did in countries at a similar income level. The impact of the Philippine depression of the 1980s is particularly evident from the failure of the country to increase its foreign trade.

Like most developing countries, South Korea began its drive for industrialization with a policy of protection against imports, but by the mid-1960s it became clear that further growth was limited by the size of the domestic market. The government then began to promote exports by subsidies, credit, and favorable exchange rates. Malaysia, where primary commodities constituted 98 percent of its total exports in 1965, managed to raise the share of manufacturing to 45 percent in 1988, although there was continued reluctance to abandon protection. Its Fifth Plan (1986–1990) projected industrial development through a strategy of export-led growth, but conceded: "Despite the provision of a series of export incentives, the [manufacturing] sector was still inclined towards production for the domestic market. This was largely due to the overall incentives being relatively attractive to import-substitution activities."[3]

Taiwan also started with an import substitution policy in 1952, but by 1960 it had reduced import restrictions and promoted exports through the establishment of export processing zones and the provision of cheap loans for exporters. Kuo and Fei have pointed out that "after the 1960s, export expansion was a decisive factor in rapid economic growth, and in the seventies its importance even outweighed domestic expansion. Economic growth due to import substitution was trivial, even though it did register a slight contribution in the sixties."[4]

Thailand was relatively slow in adopting export orientation. But by the end of the 1970s, it was becoming abundantly clear that an export policy was virtually mandatory if further economic growth were to be possible. The export of labor-intensive manufactured goods was promoted, the share of manufactures in total exports rising from 29 percent in 1980 to 52 percent in 1988. Light industrial products and processed foods are the major industrial exports, but in 1987 Thailand began to export automobiles to Canada.

The expansion of Philippine manufacturing took place behind heavily protected barriers. The result was an inefficient industry that was unable to weather the deterioration of foreign markets and contributed to the depression of 1983. Trade liberalization in 1980 had led to an inundation of imports, obliging the government to introduce quantitative import restrictions, raise import duties, and tax exports, in a desperate attempt to curb unemployment. Exports in 1988 exceeded those in 1986 by 7.3 percent, but the Philippines remained the only country in our set that did not enter an unambiguous export-oriented stage of development. Its level of protection remains higher than those prevailing in Malaysia and Thailand.

Turning to foreign assistance, its magnitudes and timing differ widely among the five countries. Taiwan was an early beneficiary of U.S. economic aid. It was a significant factor in promoting development, but it should be placed in proper perspective. From

1951 to 1961, the U.S. aid program contributed about 6 percent of GNP, on average, and provided 37 percent of gross investment. The program then fell off sharply and came to an end in 1965. Over its entire life the total of U.S. loans and grants to Taiwan amounted to almost $2.2 billion U.S. By way of comparison, South Korea received $5.930 and the Philippines $2.023 billion from 1946 to 1979.

Foreign aid was also important to South Korean development, which continued longer than that for Taiwan. From 1960 to 1969, foreign capital, including a relatively small amount invested by foreign firms, provided half of gross domestic investment. Aid continued into the seventies, although it was overshadowed by the increase in foreign investment. Aid essentially ceased after 1981 (see Table 1.6).

The magnitude of development assistance to the other three Asian countries from 1980 to 1988 is shown in the same table. The Philippines received extraordinary assistance from foreign sources after the 1983 depression to help stabilize its economy. Thailand was also the beneficiary of considerable help, although substantially below the average developing country in its income class.

Table 1.6
Official Development Assistance, 1980–1988 (millions of U.S. dollars)

	South Korea	Malaysia	Philippines	Thailand
1980	139	135	300	418
1981	330	143	376	406
1982	34	135	333	389
1983	8	177	429	431
1984	- 37	327	397	474
1985	- 9	229	486	481
1986	- 18	193	956	496
1987	11	363	770	504
1988	10	104	854	563

Source: World Bank, *World Development Report* (Washington, 1990).

Malaysia received even less, though on a per capita basis its 1988 assistance was equal to 60 percent of the Thai level.

Foreign aid contributed to economic growth in all our Asian countries, particularly Taiwan and South Korea. Among other things, it helped them get an early start. It should be pointed out, however, that many non-Asian middle-sized countries received even larger aid sums without achieving comparable economic development; among them are practically all the African countries as well as a number of countries in Central and South America. Apart from the Philippines, our Asian group appears to have used its assistance from abroad to good effect.

Military expenditures reduce the funds available for investment in growth producing resources. Three of our five countries have borne heavy defense burdens, despite which they have done well economically (see Table 1.7). South Korea and Taiwan have maintained large military establishments because of their particular circumstances—the threat of invasion by neighboring states.

Japan has a self-imposed limitation of one percent of Gross National Product (GNP) on defense expenditures, and this is sometimes offered as a partial explanation of its remarkable economic growth. Such a conclusion obviously cannot be read out of

Table 1.7
Military Expenditures, 1988–1989

	U.S. Dollars (billions)	Percent of GNP
South Korea [a]	8510	4.4
Malaysia [b]	1240	3.0
Philippines [b]	1280	2.2
Taiwan [c]	7640	5.0
Thailand [c]	1830	3.6

Source: The Heritage Foundation, *U. S. and Asia Statistical Handbook* (Washington, 1990).
[a] 1988
[b] 1989
[c] 1988/89

the foregoing data, where in fact there is a tendency toward a positive relationship between GDP growth and defense expenditures.[5] It is possible, however, that several of our Asian countries could have done even better if they had been able to maintain the Japanese level of defense.

THE POLITICAL BACKGROUND

A stable and well-managed government greatly increases the possibility of successful development. An unstable and corrupt one almost ensures economic failure. It has long been debated whether political democracy on the American or European model is optimal for developing countries, or whether a more authoritarian system is essential during the early stages of development to facilitate the adoption of policies that promise long-term benefits in return for short-term sacrifices. Favoring investment over consumption is a policy that is hard to sell in affluent countries, let alone in less developed countries where living standards are not far above subsistence levels.

The five Asian countries provide a good sample for looking at this issue. However, the analytical problem is complicated by the fact that they have had alternating mixtures of authoritarianism, usually in the form of military governments, and some degree of democracy during their developmental years. Freedom House, an American foundation, publishes an annual index of political freedom and civil liberties in which countries are rated on a scale of one (the best) to seven (the worst) on these attributes. The respective ratings for 1985 and 1990 were: South Korea and the Philippines, 4 and 2; Malaysia, 3 and 5; Taiwan, 5 and 4; and Thailand, 3 and 2. These are relatively good ratings; with few exceptions, only the industrialized nations rate higher.

A brief description of the evolution of political power during the past three or four decades may contribute to an understanding of the changes in the political systems of the five countries. The course of South Korean politics during these years has been described by Nick Eberstadt as follows:

In the four decades between 1949 and 1987, the ROK experienced not a single peaceful and orderly transfer of political power. One president was turned out of office by riots; another came to power in a putsch and ruled until he was assassinated by a trusted aide; a third consolidated his position after leading what came to be called a "constitutional coup."[6]

This may be overly simplistic. There were important differences among the various political phases, particularly with respect to economic policy. Prior to the Korean civil war, a nationalist movement under Syngman Rhee was able to win out over left-wing forces. The American occupation authorities attempted to impose some democratic reforms, but the outbreak of war enabled Rhee to consolidate his power by developing his Liberal party into a corporatist organization. Business enterprises that contributed to the Liberal party received favors, and the nascent labor movement was placed under strict government control.

Growing government corruption and rioting eventually led to Rhee's resignation. A short-lived republic attempted to democratize the system, but conflict among its supporters led to its gradual disintegration, and it was eventually overturned by a military coup led by Park Chung-lee. During its first three years in office, the Park administration established an economic planning board and began working on a development plan. A modicum of democracy was introduced in 1964 when Park was elected to the presidency. Major reforms were subsequently undertaken, including liberalization of the economy, an emphasis on exports, and better conditions for foreign investment. Labor unions were permitted to operate, though under continuing government control.

Park was reelected by a narrow margin in 1971, but the strong showing of the opposition led him to declare a state of emergency and install martial law. The constitution was suspended, the universities were closed, and all political parties were banned. Park's assassination in 1979 and the installation of Chun Doo Hwan as his successor led to a continuation of authoritarian rule. It was not until 1987 that for the first time in its modern political history, South Korea enjoyed a genuinely competitive race for the presidency.

The political situation in South Korea in 1990, three years after Roh Tae Woo, a retired general and a close friend of Chun Doo Hwan, was sworn in as president, has been described in the following terms:

> By and large, Koreans are free to write and say what they think. Three years ago they were not. By and large, Korean workers get paid a wage that reflects their work. Three years ago they did not. Korea has not collapsed into an anarchy of petrol bombs and tear-gas, as some feared it would. Nor has the army tried to take back the power it relinquished in 1987. Few countries with dictatorships so recent in their histories can boast as much.[7]

If democracy is defined as the rule of law, including the protection of individual rights, due process, freedom of speech, and the right to organize political opposition to the government in power, South Korea has not had much of it during the past 40 years. This is not to say that all regimes have been equally oppressive, for there have been swings over time. South Korean dependence on the United States for military support and export outlets have also tended to reduce blatant antidemocratic actions that might have inflamed American public opinion against South Korea.

Would South Korea's economic growth have been more rapid if a greater degree of political democracy had prevailed? South Korean growth rates were remarkably high as things stood, but of course they could have been even higher. Japan, for example, did very well indeed with a democratic system. There is no simple answer to the South Korean question, particularly in view of the fact that the policies followed by some of the authoritarian regimes followed correct economic policies. A World Bank study gives high grades to pre-Roh export policies:

> There is little doubt about either the main directions of or chief ac-
> complishments of Korea's development strategy. While Korea's export
> "takeoff" started from an unusually low base, and was supported by a

general expansion of world trade, it would not have been possible without decisive and innovative policies. These included a rationalized exchange rate regime, strong export incentives, selective import liberalization, directed credit, and a host of finely tuned, export-promoting instruments.[8]

Taiwan also experienced authoritarian rule for most of the postwar years, but under quite different circumstances. A single political party, the Kuomintang, which Chiang Kai-shek had brought with him when he was defeated by the communists on the Mainland, controlled the country for the entire period, supported by a strong military establishment. There was a gradual loosening of the political bonds during the eighties. Opposition parties were permitted to operate and challenge the Kuomintang in elections. However, although the authority of the Kuomintang has been reduced, it still retains control of the parliament, and full democracy has not been restored.

The interesting thing about the political scene in Taiwan, however, was the sharp dichotomy between political and economic administration. Chiang turned over control of economic policy to a group of technocrats, many of whom had advanced degrees in the physical sciences. C. K. Yen, who over a period of three decades held the positions of minister of finance, prime minister, and president of the republic, began his career as a professor of chemistry in China. K. T. Li, who was minister of economic affairs and of finance for more than a decade, was trained as a physicist in Britain. Y. S. Sun, who held the economic affairs portfolio before becoming prime minister, was an electrical engineer.

This remarkable group of people and their colleagues provided consistent and generally sound economic policy guidance, and made a major contribution to Taiwan's economic development. Chiang also brought in as consultants a number of Chinese-American academic economists, among them T. C. Liu, listened to what they had to say, and often acted on their advice. It is probably true that no other postwar developing country had so many highly trained people in policy positions. Taiwan cannot be classified as a democracy, but "technocracy" might be an appropriate characterization.

Though Malaysia enjoyed a substantial degree of democracy after it gained its independence from Britain in 1957, ethnic conflict prevented the country from enjoying the full fruits of the system. Events began auspiciously even before independence; the first federal elections, which were held in 1955, were dominated by an alliance of the three major ethnic groups, which won all but one seat in the legislature. The United Malays National Organization represented the Malay majority, which constituted 47 percent of the population; the Chinese (34 percent) were represented by the Malayan Chinese Association; and the 9 percent of Indians by the Malayan Indian Congress.[9]

The constitution that was adopted provided special privileges for the Malays, concessions that the minority groups were obliged to make in order to gain citizenship and the right to participate in the political process. Government administration was largely in the hands of the Malays, who also provided the manpower for the rubber plantations and the tin mines, while private manufacturing and trade were dominated by Chinese and Indian businessmen who enjoyed a large measure of independence from government regulation.

The period of ethnic truce came to an abrupt end in 1969. The Malays complained that their economic interests were not being protected. Their per capita income averaged half that of the Chinese. In elections held in 1969, the Malays failed for the first time to gain the two-thirds parliamentary majority necessary to change the constitution. Rioting broke out in Kuala Lumpur, resulting in many deaths and a great deal of property destruction, most of it Chinese. A state of emergency was declared and parliament was suspended, replaced by a National Operations Council.

Parliamentary government was restored in 1971, but the constitution was amended to prohibit ar y discussion of sensitive issues, including special privileges for Malays. A New Economic Policy had been adopted a year earlier, setting forth specific targets for Malay ownership of enterprises; they were to own at least 30 percent of corporate equities by 1990. They were also assigned minimum quotas in manufacturing employment, university enrollment, and managerial positions. This was affirmative action with a vengeance, but in favor of the majority rather than the minority. It also marked a break with the previous policy of noninterference in the conduct of economic affairs. The government began to sponsor Malay-operated enterprises, and purchased stock of foreign-owned companies to reduce the large foreign share of the economy that was a holdover from the colonial period.

Redistribution of ownership might have been expected to impede development, but economic growth continued. However, there were special circumstances that favored the economy. Large deposits of oil were discovered and, by 1977, 200,000 barrels of oil a day were being produced. The prices of Malaysia's other raw material exports rose. These fortuitous events concealed rising tensions within the private sector that arose from the imposition of strict licensing regulations affecting the Chinese-owned enterprises, the result of which was a reduction in private domestic as well as foreign investment.

Twenty years of sustained growth came to an end in 1984 when a severe depression occurred as a result of falling world prices for rubber, palm oil, and tin. The national product actually declined for two years. Beginning in 1987, recovery set in, and by 1988 the country was once more on a rapid growth path. The government, which had reacted against the depression by financing heavy industry, reversed itself and not only deemphasized large-scale government projects but began to privatize some government-owned enterprises.

The events of 1969 and its aftermath aside, Malaysia has enjoyed a long period of political stability. This might have been more conducive to economic advance had it not been for the consequences of the country's ethnic divisions. The government accorded priority to the objective of increasing Malay participation in the ownership and management of industry, not always with favorable results. This sometimes entailed diversion of scarce resources to subsidies for public enterprises and education that could have been better employed elsewhere. Concentration on restructuring society in favor of one ethnic group marred what might otherwise have been a relatively democratic political system.

Thailand, by way of contrast, has had a long history of political instability, with one military regime succeeding another. There was a brief interlude in 1973, when a military leadership was overthrown following a bloody repression of a student demonstration. A caretaker civilian government drafted a new constitution and held elections, but it was unable to cope with a wave of protests by labor and other groups. New elections in 1975 were held against a background of open conflict between left- and right-wing parties. The military stepped in once again in 1976, abrogated constitutional government, and established martial law.

There followed a decade of what might be called semi-parliamentary government, supervised by the military. In 1980, Field Marshal Prem Tinsulanon, who had earlier been minister of defense, assumed the post of prime minister, which he continued to occupy for eight years. In a surprising move, he dissolved the parliament in 1988, ordered new elections, and declined to remain in office. General Chatichai Choonhavan, his successor, became the first popularly elected prime minister in many years. He was initially regarded as a transition leader coming after a powerful predecessor, but he acted quickly to take domestic and foreign initiatives.

But despite the achievement of record rates of economic growth—the GDP rose by 11 percent in 1988 and 1989—the Chatichai administration was overthrown by a military coup in 1991, ending another brief period of civilian rule. The military junta that took control committed itself to holding general elections and the restoration of civilian government, but when this is to take place is uncertain at the present writing.

The Philippines gained their independence from the United States after World War II, and for almost two decades, a relatively democratic system prevailed. In 1953 Ramon Magsaysay was elected president by an overwhelming majority, and it seemed as though democratic institutions were firmly rooted, with a well-functioning two-party system. Magsaysay died in a plane crash in 1957, and was succeeded by Carlos Garcia, who lost the 1961 election to Diosdado Macapagal.

The man who was most closely involved with the course of economic development in the Philippines was Ferdinand Marcos, who came to power legitimately in 1965, and was reelected four years later in an election marked by fraud and violence. Facing a constitutional bar to a third term, he declared martial law in 1972 and effectively brought Philippine democracy to a halt. He closed down the congress and jailed many of his opponents. He lifted martial law in 1981 and permitted elections, which he won handily. Widespread corruption and failure to distribute the fruits of growth more equitably led to growing discontent. The assassination of his principal political opponent, Benigno Aquino, marked the beginning of the end for Marcos. The 1986 presidential campaign was chaotic, with both Marcos and Aquino's wife, Corazon, claiming victory. When the military turned against Marcos and refused to suppress demonstrations against him, he fled to Hawaii, and Mrs. Aquino became president.

She subsequently held elections under a new constitution and achieved great popularity. But the Marcos heritage continued to haunt her: a huge foreign debt, an inefficient bureaucracy, and continued corruption. There have been a number of unsuccessful coups against her. Little has been done to improve conditions for the large poverty population. Mrs. Aquino announced that she would not run for office when her term expires in 1992, thus further limiting her power to effect changes. Her great achievement has been in restoring democracy to a country that had languished under a venal dictatorship for two decades. There can be little doubt that a good deal of the blame for the failures of the Philippine economy can be laid at the door of Ferdinand Marcos.

For the future, democracy is not well rooted in the Philippines. Anticipated economic growth of 4 to 5 percent during the next few years will do little more than provide the possibility of jobs for projected increases in the labor force. Corruption has not disappeared, despite Mrs. Aquino's efforts. Her successors are likely to be challenged by wealthy groups seeking privileges common in the past. An observer of the Philippine scene has noted that "there is a distinct possibility of cycles between authoritarian and 'democratic' governments in the 1990s."[10]

This brief review of political events in the five Asian countries does not provide the basis for any definitive evaluation of what form of government is most likely to further economic development. Taiwan prospered despite the lack of representative government, as did South Korea. Thailand and Malaysia were able to achieve satisfactory growth rates, the former mainly under military rule, the latter despite continuing ethnic conflict.

What seems to have been of greater importance than the precise form of government was continuity and acceptance of expert advice, as well as relative freedom from corruption. Among the crucial decisions that had to be made were the extent to which the private sector was to be permitted to operate independently, and the openness of borders to foreign trade and investment. These decisions do not appear to have been correlated with any particular type of administration. It can be argued that democracy on the Western model is a good in itself and should be adopted by developing countries on that account alone. But it would not be easy to sustain the position that four of the five countries in our sample would have achieved more rapid economic growth under genuinely parliamentary regimes.

NOTES

1. World Bank, *Korea: Managing the Industrial Transition* (Washington, 1987), p. 31.

2. Rudiger Dornbusch and Yung Chul Park, "Korean Growth Policy," *Brookings Papers on Economic Activity*, 1987, vol. 2, Washington, pp. 412–13.

3. Malaysia, *Fifth Malaysian Plan 1986–1990* (Kuala Lumpur, 1986), p. 337.

4. Shirley W. Y. Kuo and John C. H. Fei, "Causes and Roles of Export Expansion in the Republic of China," in Walter Galenson (editor), *Foreign Trade and Investment* (Madison: University of Wisconsin Press, 1985), p. 67.

5. For a general discussion of the relationship between military expenditures and economic growth see David B. H. Denoon, editor, *Constraints on Strategy* (McLean, VA: Pergamon Brassey's, 1986).

6. Nick Eberstadt, "Democracy and Development in East Asia," *National Affairs* (Fall 1989): p. 80.

7. *The Economist*, August 18, 1990, Survey, p. 5.

8. World Bank, *Korea*, p. 29.

9. The data are as of 1975. The remaining 10 percent consist of various indigenous groups.

10. Manuel Montes, "The Philippine Economy in the 1990s: Recovery and Restoration," in *Problems of Developing Countries in the 1990s*, Vol. 2 (Washington: World Bank, 1990), p. 167.

2

The Labor Force

At early stages of development, land and labor are the most abundant factors of production and the main resources available for economic growth. Capital becomes more available as the economy develops, and greater proportions of it are utilized in the production process. Labor intensity, the mode of production that relies primarily on labor, gives way to capital intensity, and agriculture yields to industry. The history of economic development points to the inexorable rise of the machine, first in industry—manufacturing, transportation, energy—and then in the service sector.

Population growth has had a bad name in the postwar world. It is argued that developing countries have not been able to match it with sufficient economic growth to prevent a fall in per capita income and greater impoverishment. Investment in birth control is seen as yielding a greater marginal product than other forms of investment. As Malthus had predicted, the population outruns the food supply and the consequence is famine.

It is useful, in the context of the present study, to look at the experience of a group of countries that have had no difficulty es-

Table 2.1
Average Annual Growth of Population, 1965–1988 (percent)

	1965–80	1980–88
South Korea [a]	2.0	1.2
Malaysia [b]	2.5	2.0
Philippines [b]	2.9	2.5
Taiwan [a]	2.3	1.4
Thailand [b]	2.9	1.9
Lower middle income countries [b]	2.5	2.3
Upper middle income countries [a]	2.0	1.8

Sources: World Bank, *World Development Report* (Washington, 1990); Republic of China, *Statistical Yearbook* (Taipei, 1989), Table 1.
[a]$2290–$5420 (1988 prices)
[b]$1380–$2160 (1988 prices)

caping the Malthusian trap. Table 2.1 shows the rate of population growth for our five countries over two periods—1965 to 1980 and 1980 to 1988, together with the average rates for all middle-income countries. The populations of the five Asian countries increased as rapidly or more rapidly than the generality of developing countries in their income class from 1965 to 1980. For the later period (1980 to 1988) in every case except for the Philippines, the Asian country rates were well below those of the other developing countries. This illustrates a well established principle: As industrialization and urbanization proceed, and as income rises, population growth tends to slow. Taiwan and South Korea provide particularly dramatic examples of this tendency.

Bringing together GNP and population growth produces the results shown in Table 2.1 above. Per capita GNP growth for four of the five countries far outdistanced that of the average developing country. Only the Philippines lagged behind, not so much because of an excessive increase in population, but because of insufficient economic growth.

The best index of labor input into the production process is the labor force, the proportion of the total population engaged in gainful employment. Labor-force growth data from 1965 to 1985, together with projections to the year 2000, appear in Table 2.2. Taiwan and Malaysia had extraordinarily high rates for both periods, and all the Asian countries showed up well in comparison with the developing country averages. Here the Philippines were close to average, suggesting that factors other than labor input were responsible for its lagging growth. Unemployment, discussed below, is one such factor, since the unemployed are included in the labor force but do not contribute to production.

Manpower can be a valuable productive input rather than an obstacle to development. There is one critical proviso: it must be used productively. This does not mean that it is necessarily highly skilled or engaged in capital-intensive processes. The general rule, which is often followed more in the breach than in the observance, is that labor and capital should be employed in that combination in which the marginal productivity of the two are equal. If labor is

Table 2.2
Average Annual Growth of the Labor Force, 1965–1985 (percent)

	1965-1980	1980-1985	1985-2000 (projected)
South Korea [a]	2.8	2.7	1.9
Malaysia [b]	3.4	2.9	2.6
Philippines [b]	2.5	2.5	2.4
Taiwan [a]	3.5	2.8	n.a.
Thailand [b]	2.8	2.5	1.7
Lower middle income countries [b]	2.4	2.6	2.5
Upper middle income countries [a]	2.6	2.3	2.3

Sources: World Bank, *World Development Report* (Washington, 1988), Table 31; Republic of China, *Taiwan Statistical Data Book* (Taipei, 1989).
[a]$2290–$5420 (1988 dollars)
[b]$1380–$2160 (1988 dollars)

more productive at the margin than capital, it should be preferred even if the result is viewed as "backward" in some sense. To introduce modern machinery and equipment when its intended output can be produced more cheaply by labor is a waste of resources.

LABOR-FORCE PARTICIPATION

A growing population does not necessarily imply a growing labor force. The link between them is the participation rate, the proportion of people out of a given population who are working or seeking work. This rate varies considerably from country to country, depending on such factors as age structure, the availability of paid employment, and local customs, among other things. In general, a higher ratio represents a fuller utilization of the population for productive purposes.

Table 2.3 shows the labor-force participation rates for the five Asian countries for the last 25 to 30 years, for the population aged 15 to 64 years. There was not much change over the period for South Korea, Malaysia, and Taiwan. There was a sharp drop in the Philippines in the most recent estimate, reflecting the depression of the 1980s. Thailand is a special case, with its very high participa-

Table 2.3
Labor Force Participation Rates[a]

	25 to 30 years ago	15 to 20 years ago	Most recent estimate
South Korea	63.4	63.1	62.1
Malaysia	66.9	67.0	66.7
Philippines	71.9	68.4	62.3
Taiwan [b]	58.2	58.3	60.1
Thailand	95.3	93.6	83.6

Sources: World Bank, *Social Indicators of Development* (Washington, 1989); Republic of China, *Taiwan Statistical Data Book* (Taipei, 1989), Table 28.
[a]Ratio of the labor force aged 15 to 64 to the population aged 15 to 64 years
[b]The data are for the years 1965, 1980, and 1989

tion rate. This is probably a function of the relative importance of agriculture in the structure of its economy. In an agricultural country most able-bodied people of working age are employed, though many of them may be unpaid family workers.

Economic development can have a number of effects on labor-force participation, not all in the same direction. A declining agricultural sector tends to lead to a reduction in overall participation (this is clear for the most recent data for Thailand), but increasing employment opportunities in manufacturing and services have an opposite effect. The rise of years of schooling that comes with growing affluence tends to reduce participation. Which effect predominates depends on the strength and rapidity of economic growth.

SECTORAL DISTRIBUTION OF THE LABOR FORCE

The distribution of the labor force by major economic sector is an index of economic development. Normally, a large proportion of the labor force is engaged in agricultural pursuits at early stages of development. The industrial sector gains at the expense of agriculture with economic growth as workers move from the farms to urban jobs. In mature economies, the service sector expands and eventually becomes the largest of the three. Not all countries follow this precise sequence; for example, farm workers may move directly into the services. But the general pattern holds true for most countries.

The data in Table 2.4 illustrate the course of sectoral employment in the five Asian countries. In the course of almost a quarter of a century, the industrial share of employment doubled in South Korea and Taiwan, while that of Malaysia increased by almost 50 percent. Only 13 percent of Taiwan's labor force were engaged in agricultural pursuits in 1989, a lower figure than that found in most Latin American countries and in some European countries as well.

Table 2.4
Distribution of Employment, by Major Economic Sector, 1965–1987
(percent of total employment)

	Agriculture			Industry			Services		
	1965	1980	1987	1965	1980	1987	1965	1980	1987
South Korea	55	36	20	15	27	34	30	37	46
Malaysia	59	42	32	13	19	23	29	39	45
Philippines	58	52	45	16	16	16	26	33	39
Taiwan	47	20	13	22	42	42	31	38	45
Thailand	82	71	64	5	10	13	13	19	24

Sources: World Bank, *World Development Report* (Washington, 1988); International Labor Office, *Yearbook of Labor Statistics* (Geneva, 1990); Republic of China, *Yearbook of Manpower Statistics* (Taipei, 1989), Table 33.

Service sector employment was already substantial in four of the five countries in 1965. Part of this may be attributed to what is sometimes called traditional employment: domestic service, repair work, small shops, primitive transportation. As development proceeds, many of these people manage to secure more productive work in the service sector itself rather than moving into manufacturing. By 1989, the service sector was larger than industry in South Korea and Malaysia, but industry held its own in Taiwan, a situation that will change as industrial productivity rises.

The experience of Thailand and the Philippines merits special comment. As noted above, Thailand retained a large agricultural sector in 1987 despite a favorable rate of economic growth. The country was overwhelmingly agricultural at the outset of development, and industry started from a very low base. A considerable amount of wooded land had remained available so that families could clear it and grow crops instead of migrating to the cities in search of work. For most of the 1970s, farm prices were high, and a good living could be made from the land. But with gradually diminishing available land and falling crop prices during the following decade there would probably have been a more rapid move into industry had it not been for the character of the new manufacturing sector:

> The manufacturing sector has never played anything like the same role as an engine of growth . . . as it did in Taiwan and the Republic of Korea. Many of Thailand's industries are still relatively inefficient and dependent on support or disguised subsidies from the government. There is a heavy reliance on imported equipment, technology and raw materials, while much of Thailand's industry tends to be capital-intensive rather than labor-intensive.[1]

As for the Philippines, despite average GDP growth of 5.9 percent over the period 1965 to 1980, the employment share of industry remained unchanged. The explanation again appears to have been a bias toward capital-intensive industries, even more marked than in the case of Thailand. It took the form of heavy protection against imports and other incentives that encouraged the production of indigenous capital goods that should have been imported from industrial nations, and the stifling of potential export industries that could have been based on cheap Philippine labor.[2]

The experience of the five Asian countries demonstrates that favorable rates of economic growth alone do not constitute a sufficient condition for putting a country on a balanced development path. Industrialization in disregard of relative factor costs can have negative long-run consequences, even though they may appear to produce immediate gains. Once established, inefficient and inappropriate enterprises are difficult to eliminate because of economic as well as political consequences. Propping them up by government subsidies only compounds the damage by acting as a drag on further development.

The failure of the industrial labor force to expand as the GDP rises should be taken as a signal of erroneous policy decisions. There are exceptions, particularly where development is fueled by agricultural expansion and modernization. The experience of the Ivory Coast, at least up to 1980, provides an example. In the long run, however, the doubling of the industrial labor force in two dec-

Table 2.5
Nonagricultural Employment, by Major Industry, 1965–1989 (percent of total nonagricultural employment)

	South Korea 1989	Malaysia 1988	Philippines 1989	Taiwan 1988	Thailand 1986
Mining	1.0	0.9	1.3	0.3	0.6
Manufacturing	34.3	22.9	19.2	39.0	25.1
Electricity, gas, water	0.1	1.2	0.7	0.5	1.4
Construction	8.1	9.1	7.6	8.7	7.4
Trade, restaurants, hotels	26.6	25.1	25.6	22.4	29.5
Communications, transport	6.2	6.3	9.1	6.3	6.3
Finance, real estate	6.1	5.1	3.3	4.3	a
Community, school and professional services	17.6	29.3	33.1	18.5	29.8

Sources: International Labor Office, *Yearbook of Labor Statistics* (Geneva, 1990); Republic of China, *Yearbook of Manpower Statistics* (Taipei, 1989), Table 33.
[a]Included in community, school, and professional services

ades, as exemplified by Taiwan and South Korea, provides a developmental model that offers greater chance of success.

A subsectoral breakdown of nonagricultural employment in the five Asian countries appears in Table 2.5, for the latest available years. The final category—community, school, and professional services (in one case combined with financial and real estate services, a relatively small item), includes government employment, and is of particular interest. The Philippines are at the top, reflecting the large bureaucracy of the Marcos years. Taiwan and South Korea had the lowest proportion of employment in this subsector. This illustrates a tendency on the part of

developing countries to attempt to create employment through the
public sector when there are not sufficient manufacturing jobs.

WOMEN IN THE LABOR FORCE

Participation rates for men and women separately appear in
Table 2.6. (The rates for Taiwan are relatively understated because of definitional differences.) They represent the labor force
of each sex as a proportion of its share in the total population.
For all countries except the Philippines, the male rates rose
between 1965 and 1987 and ended up fairly close to one another.
The female rates increased more rapidly than the male, except
again for the Philippines, and for Thailand, where they were
already high in 1965.

The overall figures conceal shifts in the composition of female
employment that took place as a result of increased employment
opportunities. Data for individual countries make this clear. Table
2.7 shows changes in the classification of female jobs between
1963 and 1989. In South Korea, a large number of women moved

Table 2.6
Labor Force Participation Rates, by Sex, 1965 and 1987[a]

	South Korea	Malaysia	Philippines	Taiwan [b]	Thailand
Male					
1965	48	47	49	43	52
1987	53	51	49	50	56
Female					
1965	20	20	25	18	47
1987	28	28	24	33	48

Sources: World Bank, Social Indicators of Development (Washington, 1988); Republic
of China, Taiwan Statistical Data Book (Taipei, 1988).
[a]Percentage of population of all ages in the labor force
[b]The figures for Taiwan are relatively understated because the labor force includes only
persons 15 years of age and over, while for the other countries, persons of all ages
who are working are counted as participants

Table 2.7
Employment of Women, by Personal Status, 1963–1989 (percent of total)

	South Korea 1963	South Korea 1989	Malaysia 1963	Malaysia 1989	Taiwan 1963	Taiwan 1989	Thailand 1987
Unpaid family workers	75.2	25.1	16	24	48.4	17.7	54.6
Employers	-	-	4	-	1.2	1.3	0.8
Self-employed	17.4	18.9	27	17	11.8	8.9	19.2
Regular employees	7.8	56.0	53	59	38.6	72.1	25.4
Private	-	-	-	-	28.6	61.8	20.3
Public	-	-	-	-	10.0	10.3	5.1

Sources: Korea: Jang-ho Kim, *Wages, Employment, and Income Distribution in South Korea* (New Delhi: ARTEP, 1986); International Labor Office, *Yearbook of Labor Statistics*, (Geneva, 1990). Malaysia: Saw Swee Hock, *Changing Labor Force of Malaysia* (Quezon: Council for Asian Manpower Studies, 1984), p. 18; International Labor Office, *Yearbook of Labor Statistics* (Geneva, 1990). Taiwan: Republic of China, *Yearbook of Manpower Statistics* (Taipei, 1989), Table 36. Thailand: International Labor Office, *Yearbook of Labor Statistics* (Bangkok, 1990).

from work within the family into self-employment outside the home. The number of employed female workers rose substantially, but remained a relatively small proportion of the total in 1989.

The shift in Taiwan was of the same nature but more rapid. Over a period of two decades, the proportion of unpaid female family workers in the labor force fell by almost two-thirds, most of them moving into paid employment. The Malaysian record manifests the same tendency, though the change was not as great as in Taiwan.

A more disaggregated picture of the female contribution to economic development can be gained from Tables 2.8 and 2.9. The first of these tables shows changes in the distribution of women workers among major subsectors of the economy. The proportion engaged in agriculture declined in every country, particularly in South Korea and Taiwan, where manufacturing was the principal

Table 2.8
Percentage Distribution of Women Employees in the Economically Active Population, 1970 and 1989

	South Korea		Malaysia		Philippines		Taiwan		Thailand	
	1970	1989	1970	1989	1970	1989	1970	1989	1970	1989
Agriculture	58.9	21.7	49.5	30.8	31.4	30.9	40.6	9.9	82.7	64.6
Mining	0.2	0.1	0.8	0.2	0.1	0.2	0.4	0.1	0.3	0.2
Manufacturing	14.3	28.9	8.0	20.2	19.4	13.6	22.5	38.1	3.7	9.2
Construction	0.6	1.6	0.4	0.8	0.1	0.2	0.5	2.3	0.3	0.9
Electric, gas	0.1	-	-	-	-	0.1	0.1	0.1	-	0.2
Commerce	14.2[a]	27.7	5.5	19.7	12.0	25.2	15.0	22.5	6.0	12.9
Transportation	-	1.0	0.4	1.2	0.3	0.7	1.8	2.1	0.2	0.4
Services	10.2	18.9	15.3	27.1	27.5	29.0	19.1	24.9	5.4	11.7
n.e.c	1.5	-	20.1[b]	-	9.2[b]	-	-	-	1.4	-
Total	100	100	100	100	100	100	100	100	100	100

Sources: International Labor Office, *Yearbook of Labor Statistics* (Geneva, various issues); Republic of China, *Yearbook of Manpower Statistics* (Taipei, 1989), Table 12.
[a]Includes transportation
[b]Includes persons just entering the labor market

gainer. In Malaysia and Thailand, the commercial and service sectors between them absorbed more of the agriculture decline than did manufacturing.[3]

The data in Table 2.9 provide a different perspective on the role of working women; they show the changing importance of women in the labor force. Women tended to retain and even increase their relative importance in agriculture as more men moved into other sectors. The rise in their overall labor-force participation enabled them at the same time to increase their share of manufacturing employment. By the end of the 1980s, they dominated the commercial and service sectors in South Korea and Taiwan.

The Philippines are again a special case. There were more women than men engaged in manufacturing in 1970, but the situation was reversed in 1987. Between these years, the number of male workers in manufacturing increased by 73 percent, while

Table 2.9
Proportion of Women Employees in the Economically Active Population,
1970 and 1989 (percent)

	South Korea 1970 1989	Malaysia 1970 1989	Philippines 1970 1989	Taiwan 1970 1989	Thailand 1970 1989
Agriculture	41.4 45.1	36.9 35.3	19.5 24.9	33.7 28.9	49.7 45.3
Mining	7.0 9.7	12.7 11.2	5.7 10.4	8.3 16.7	26.4 30.7
Manufacturing	35.9 42.5	29.0 46.1	54.4 46.8	32.8 42.2	42.6 45.2
Construction	4.3 9.7	6.7 4.7	0.7 1.8	3.0 10.9	14.4 13.9
Electric, gas	6.5 13.6	5.0 2.8	2.9 20.5	5.9 11.4	12.0 14.8
Commerce	38.2 52.6	18.2 38.2	54.8 65.0	33.5 43.5	54.0 53.6
Transportation	7.6 8.4	4.1 9.1	2.1 4.7	10.1 14.7	6.0 8.1
Services	28.1 40.3	29.6 29.4	56.1 52.6	35.6 47.2	36.3 49.3
Total	28.9 40.7	31.8 33.3	32.0 36.3	30.9 37.7	47.1 44.7

Sources: International Labor Office, *Yearbook of Labor Statistics* (Geneva, various issues); Republic of China, *Yearbook of Manpower Statistics* (Taipei, 1989), Table 33.

the increase for women was only 25 percent. The difficulty was that the growth of manufacturing was not sufficient to absorb the 86-percent increase in the labor force. By way of contrast, South Korean manufacturing employment tripled while the increase in its total labor force was only 63 percent, with the result that large numbers of both men and women could find jobs in manufacturing. Philippine women either remained in agriculture or found work in commercial activities. It is likely that if Philippine policy had favored labor—rather than capital—intensity, more women would have found jobs in manufacturing.

The data in these tables tell a good deal about the contribution of women to economic development. By the end of the periods covered by the data, they provided between 40 and 46 percent of the labor force in manufacturing. Their importance in commercial and service activities has already been noted. If women had continued to remain at home rather than enter paid employment, the observed pattern of industrial growth would not have been possible. At the same time, for many women economic growth provided an escape from unpaid family work into paid jobs, permitting them to augment family income and widening the possibility of achieving some degree of personal independence.

OCCUPATIONAL CHANGE

Changes in the occupational structure of the labor force over a period of almost two decades are shown in Table 2.10. As expected, agricultural occupations declined in importance, while the growth of industrial occupations could also have been anticipated. The proportion of the labor force engaged in sales, clerical, and service

Table 2.10
Economically Active Population, by Occupation, 1970 and 1989 (percent of total)

	South Korea		Malaysia		Philippines		Taiwan		Thailand	
	1970	1989	1970	1989	1970	1989	1970	1989	1970	1989
Professional, technical	3.1	6.7	4.5	7.6	5.7	5.5	4.7	7.1	1.7	3.3
Administrative, management	0.9	1.4	0.7	2.0	1.2	0.9	0.4	1.0	1.5	1.5
Clerical	5.7	12.1	4.6	9.5	3.3	4.0	9.7	15.6	1.1	2.8
Sales	10.0	14.3	8.3	11.9	6.8	12.6	11.5	14.8	4.9	10.1
Service	6.5	10.5	7.8	11.8	7.6	8.1	7.3	9.0	2.8	6.3
Agricultural	49.7	18.8	46.0	30.7	53.0	40.8	36.6	12.8	78.3	64.4
Production and related	21.3	33.6	18.9	26.5	19.1	19.7	29.8	39.7	8.2	11.6
n. e.c.	2.8	2.6	9.2	–	3.3	8.6	–	–	1.5	–
Total	100	100	100	100	100	100	100	100	100	100

Sources: International Labor Office, *Yearbook of Labor Statistics* (Geneva, various issues); Republic of China, *Yearbook of Manpower Statistics* (Taipei, 1989), Table 35; Thailand, *Statistical Yearbook* (Bangkok, 1989), Table 159.

occupations uniformly increased, though at different rates. It was in the rapidly developing countries that these occupational categories tended to expand most. Notable exceptions are the doubling of the sales sector share in the Philippines and Thailand, in the case of the former undoubtedly representing expansion of the informal sector as a refuge from unemployment.

EDUCATION

Manpower skills become more important as an economy moves into the greater complexity of capital-intensive operations. But even at fairly early stages of development, some education may be essential to progress. Foreign firms setting up plants even in such labor-intensive operations as the production of electronic components have found that some secondary-school education enables employees to achieve a high level of productivity in a short time. In fact, the availability of educated manpower is a major factor in inducing multinational firms to invest in less-developed countries.

Table 2.11
Percentage of Relevant Age Group Enrolled in Educational Institutions, 1965 and 1987

	Primary [a]		Secondary		Tertiary	
	1965	1987	1965	1987	1965	1987
South Korea	101	101	35	88	6	36
Malaysia	90	102	28	59	2	7
Philippines	113	106	41	68	19	38
Taiwan	97	97	66[b]	82	11	26
Thailand	78	95	14	28	2	20

Sources: World Bank, *World Development Report* (Washington, 1990), Table 29; Republic of China, *Taiwan Statistical Data Book* (Taipei, 1988); *Statistical Yearbook* (Taipei, 1989), Table 117.
[a]For some countries with universal primary education, the enrollment ratios may exceed 100 percent because some pupils are older or younger than the standard primary school age
[b]1977

Comparative data on education are shown in Table 2.11. All five Asian countries had universal primary education by 1987, and three of the five already by 1965. South Korea and Taiwan provided some secondary education to most children of the appropriate age by 1987. Thailand, with its large farm sector, lagged behind the rest in making secondary education available.

Before considering some of the anomolies in the data, a word about the quality of education is in order. Expenditure on education might be used as a proxy for quality, but good comparative data are hard to come by, not least because of the various budgetary levels involved in financing education. A proxy that is available is the pupil-teacher ratio. Other things being equal, the lower the number of students per teacher, the greater the attention each student can receive, and the greater the prospect of learning. Student-teacher ratios are shown in Table 2.12.

There are several things that are not in accord with the hypothesis that more education leads to faster economic growth. The Philippines have done well in terms of the quantity of education, though not in quality. It has been pointed out that the Philippines had "high levels of enrollment and attainment but low levels of government support for education. This means that the quality of

Table 2.12
Student-Teacher Ratios, Primary and Secondary Education

	Primary		Secondary	
	25-30 years ago	Most recent estimate	25-30 years ago	Most recent estimate
South Korea	62	36	37	33
Malaysia	29	22	na	26
Philippines	31	32	33	na
Taiwan	42	31	25	22
Thailand	35	20	18	17

Sources: World Bank, Social Indicators of Development (Washington, 1990); Republic of China, Taiwan Statistical Data Book (Taipei, 1988).

education suffers. Precollege education is 10 years compared to the usual 12 years, and teachers are poorly paid and motivated and teaching materials and equipment obsolete and insufficient."[4]

South Korea made a tremendous leap in secondary education over the two-decade period, and this may have contributed to its economic success. However, "although the quantity of education supplied has risen, there has been little improvement in the quality—in terms of class size and pupil-teacher ratio—and middle schools in particular have deteriorated."[5] The elementary school ratio did improve considerably, but it still remained high at the close of the 1980s. The exceptionally high figure for the number of students in tertiary institutions was largely due to a reform that raised college enrollment by 30 percent in 1980.

Taiwan has invested heavily in education and attained a good level of quality, particularly with respect to its colleges and universities. There were 107 such institutions by 1987, with almost half a million students. The authorities have steered students into those disciplines most useful for development; in 1987, one-third sought engineering degrees, 11 percent were in medical and natural sciences, and 22 percent in business administration. Many students from Taiwan have received graduate degrees from American universities. A substantial proportion of these remain in the United States, but enough return to make this a profitable arrangement.[6]

Malaysia appears to have established satisfactory schooling at both the primary and secondary levels, but higher education has been hampered by ethnic conflict. Racial quotas were established for the public universities, and the Chinese minority was prevented from setting up private institutions of its own. Many Chinese students were obliged to seek a university education abroad, an expensive proposition. In 1983, there were 43,000 Malay students and 12,000 Chinese in domestic public institutions. The figures were reversed for those studying abroad: 12,000 Malays and 31,000 Chinese.[7] If domestic university slots had been made available to Chinese (and Indian) students, the low figure for Malaysia in Table 2.11 would have been much more respectable, though still below the levels for the other countries.

As for Thailand, secondary education appears to have remained less developed than might have been expected from its economic performance, but this may be a function of the rural character of the society. However, there was a sharp rise in secondary school enrollment and an expansion in the network of vocational schools and universities.

In general, all five Asian countries allocated sufficient resources to education to supply the growing needs of industry and of the service economy. Attempts to measure the precise contribution of education to development has yielded inconclusive results. Particularly at higher skill levels, where shortages are more likely to occur, the distribution of disciplines may be more important than quantity. Indeed, errors in distribution can lead to the production of skills that outstrip demand, sometimes with disastrous social consequences. The educated unemployed can constitute a dangerous political group.

UNEMPLOYMENT AND UNDEREMPLOYMENT

Both the concept and the consequences of unemployment are quite different in developed and developing countries. Developed countries have formal systems of unemployment compensation, enabling people who lose their jobs to finance the search for new ones, or to receive welfare payments if they are unsuccessful. There is a clear distinction between those who are employed and those who are not, enabling reasonably accurate estimates of prevailing unemployment levels. There are some difficulties of estimation, particularly with respect to so-called "discouraged" workers who drop out of the labor force because they do not feel that they can find a job, but the magnitude of this group can be determined.

Developing countries have little or nothing in the way of formal government support programs, so that a person who cannot find work in the regular sector must look to the traditional or informal sector in order to keep alive. The problem is less acute as long as agriculture remains the primary activity of a society, since extended family arrangements can generally be counted on. When people flock to the cities, this system may break down, and everyone must find something to do.

The problem then becomes one of underemployment rather than unemployment, and this is difficult to define. Informal sector jobs are generally characterized by low income and correspondingly low productivity, but using either of these criteria as a definition is complicated by the fact that earnings in the formal sector are often low as well. Nor are hours of work a good criterion, since many people in the informal sector must work long hours to eke out a living wage.

With these cautions in mind, let us examine the available unemployment data shown in Table 2.13. Though the International Labor Office (ILO), which attempts to compile unemployment figures, tries to persuade member countries to adopt uniform standards and adhere to them, there is no guarantee that this is done. The ILO simply accepts and prints the data that are submitted to it, and hopes that they have some relation to reality.

The statistics in Table 2.13 suggest rates of unemployment that would be remarkably low even in developed nations. If the figures are accurate, South Korea, Taiwan, and Thailand appear to have only fractional levels of unemployment at most, while the somewhat higher rates shown for Malaysia and the Philippines would not be unwelcome in many high-income countries.

Supplementary data may help clarify the picture for the individual countries. South Korean unemployment in 1983 was reported to be 4.1 percent. In the same year, 34.6 percent of all those employed were in the urban traditional sector and 29.7 percent were in the rural traditional sector.[8] Of course, this does not mean that all of these employees were underemployed, but many were undoubtedly doing marginally productive work. The unemployment data may have covered only those employed in the modern sector.

What can be said is that at the onset of the industrialization drive that began in the early 1960s, the South Korean labor market was characterized by an abundance of labor, most of it unskilled. Thirty

Table 2.13
Unemployment Rates, 1978–1989 (percent)

	South Korea	Malaysia	Philippines	Taiwan	Thailand
1978	3.2	–	4.0	1.7	0.9
1979	3.8	–	3.5	1.3	1.0
1980	5.2	5.6	4.8	1.2	0.8
1981	4.5	–	5.4	1.4	1.3
1982	4.4	–	5.5	2.1	2.8
1983	4.1	–	4.9	2.7	2.9
1984	3.8	–	7.0	2.4	2.9
1985	4.0	6.9	6.1	2.9	2.6
1986	3.8	8.3	6.4	2.7	3.5
1987	3.1	8.2	9.1	2.0	5.8
1988	2.5	8.1	8.3	1.7	–
1989	2.6	–	8.4	1.6	–

Sources: International Labor Office, *Yearbook of Labor Statistics* (Geneva 1988); Republic of China, *Statistical Yearbook* (Taipei, 1989), Table 22; Malaysia, *Yearbook of Statistics* (Kuala Lumpur, 1988), Table 9–1; Thailand, (1966 and 1967), *Statistical Yearbook* (Bangkok, 1989), Table 156.

years later, the pool of cheap labor was gone, and labor-intensive industries had begun to move offshore. However, agriculture still provided employment for 21 percent of the labor force, while 51 percent were in services. The share of manufacturing had doubled over the 30-year period, but labor reserves remained adequate to fuel its expansion.

There has been some talk of an actual shortage of labor, and some firms have actually petitioned the government to admit foreign workers. However, what shortage actually prevails appears to be due to a maldistribution of labor, both geographic and by industry.

Taiwan's experience has been similar. Unemployment rose during the 1950s as population growth exceeded the demand for labor. By the mid-1970s various groups that are often characterized by unemployment—unpaid family workers, people working on their own account, short-time employees—had shrunk considerably.

But a decade later, there were still enough people in nonregular jobs to give rise to the following comment:

> The official indicator has frequently been criticized for understating actual unemployment since it doesn't reflect underemployment among the some 20 percent of workers who are 'self-employed,' a category which includes street hawkers getting by between jobs; college graduates, among whom the underemployment rate is estimated by some officials at 16 to 22 percent; and the 35 percent of the labor force employed in family businesses.[9]

The other side of the coin is that a shortage of unskilled labor has led to illegal immigration. Estimates of the number of foreign workers in Taiwan range from 20,000 to 140,000. The government is considering regularization of labor from out of the country for public construction projects, which have been particularly hard hit. It might also be pointed out that many of those employed in family firms are hardly underemployed. They often work long hours. Some underemployment undoubtedly exists, but Taiwan has left the ranks of developing countries in this respect.

Efforts to measure unemployment in Thailand provide a textbook example of the difficulties involved in securing reasonable estimates in developing countries.[10] It was acknowledged that the official unemployment data, based upon labor force surveys, did not present an adequate picture of the real situation. Beginning in 1977, the survey counted, in addition to the fully employed, those "underutilized by hours worked," those "underutilized by income," and those "underutilized by mismatch" (of job qualifications).

The mismatch category was dropped because most employment was in agriculture, where special skills did not play an important role. The low-income category was also dropped because of the difficulty of determining an appropriate cutoff point; small changes in the income level chosen had large effects on the number classified as underemployed. The number of hours worked remains as the only underemployment criterion, and this turned out not to be very significant in urban areas, where there were very few who worked less than 20 hours a week in a setting in which 75 percent of all workers put in more than 50 hours a week.

The exercise proved more successful in measuring seasonal unemployment in agriculture. Surveys indicated that the farm labor force fluctuated in the range of 4 to 7 million people between the slack and peak seasons. The 1983 first-quarter rate of rural unemployment would have been 16.5 percent rather than 8 percent if the seasonally inactive labor force was included. Thus the official overall 1983 rate of unemployment—2.9 percent—may have reflected the situation among the relatively small number of regular employees in urban areas, but it did not take rural conditions into account.

The ILO statistical yearbooks, from which unemployment data for the other countries (except Taiwan) were drawn, do not carry the relevant Malaysian data. The rates shown in Table 2.13, derived from another source, reveal the existence of relatively high unemployment, which was reported to be three times as high for the 15- to 24-year age group. First time job seekers constituted 50 percent of the unemployed, and about half of these had to wait a year or more before finding a job. To generate more employment opportunities, the government planned to undertake labor-intensive programs in the form of building rural infrastructure and financing small scale industry during the period 1986–1990. Self-employment was to be stimulated in urban areas by legalizing the hawking of goods and setting up more market places.[11]

Along with a general surplus of labor, there were some skill-specific manpower shortages, including electronic technicians, machine fitters, blacksmiths, sheet metal workers, and cabinet makers. At the same time, college graduates were having difficulty finding suitable employment. Structural imbalance of this nature is fairly typical of developing countries, where the children of affluent families have a strong preference for university education over vocational training for the skilled crafts.

An article dealing with the unemployment situation in the Philippines has the following to say: "The Philippine unemployment problem has always been massive. The low unemployment rates, ranging from 4 to 6 percent, given by the National Census and Statistics Office . . . in the 1970s were never believed even in official circles although these were often cited by the Marcos regime to give the country a false sense of economic stability."[12] To make matters worse, underemployment has been endemic. An official source that carried an unemployment rate of 4.6 percent for 1983 also carried an underemployment rate of 30.1 percent, consisting of 15.5 percent for visible and 14.6 percent for hidden underemployment.[13]

As has already been pointed out, one of the principal causes of Philippine unemployment was the failure of the manufacturing sector to absorb the rapidly growing labor force. During the 1980s, traditional manufactures were hit by high taxes and interest rates and by the importation of lower priced goods following trade liberalization. Some of the more modern industries suffered from a lack of foreign exchange with which to import needed materials. A World Bank study criticized efforts to stabilize the economy through restriction of imports and taxation of exports, and urged that government spending be reduced.[14]

The plight of the Philippines stands in sharp contrast to the ability of its neighbors to leave the ranks of countries with an "unlimited supply of labor," to use Arthur Lewis' term. South Korea and Taiwan sopped up their pools of underemployed farm labor and have been running into labor shortages. Malaysia and Thailand still have labor reserves in agriculture, but their farm production is sufficiently profitable to foreclose unstructured migration to the cities. The large surplus of labor in the Philippines would be a favorable development factor if it could be employed efficiently. Failure to do this would not only limit growth, but might also aggravate an already unstable political situation.

LABOR PRODUCTIVITY

Increased labor inputs are an important source of economic growth. The efficiency with which labor is applied in producing goods and services may be an even more important factor. The same is true of capital; thus to secure a complete picture of growth dynamics, we should secure measures of change in total factor productivity, that is, the productivity of capital as well as of labor.

The difficulty of securing adequate data is one of measurement rather than conception. Labor-input statistics are readily available, but capital inputs are much more difficult to calculate. There are estimates for some developed countries, but no standardized internationally comparative data. We therefore limit the analysis to labor productivity, an older and more widely studied concept.

Labor productivity may rise for a number of reasons. Greater effort on the part of workers is one, but not the most important. The skills that are employed have a significant effect on output, and it is the purpose of education and training to raise them. The quantity and quality of the capital equipment with which people work may have an even greater impact on productivity.

The labor productivity data most readily available are for the manufacturing sector. In principle, it would be very helpful to determine service productivity as well, but measurement problems intrude once again. Labor inputs into services are available, but determining the output of many services—for example, government, health, many personal services—raises conceptual problems.

Indexes of labor productivity in manufacturing are shown in Table 2.14. Apart from the Philippines, all the countries experienced respectable productivity increases over the period covered. In making international comparisons, two things must be kept in mind. The first has to do with the inception of the process of industrialization. Starting from a small base, early gains are apt to be large, while as industry develops the rate of increase tends to diminish. South Korea and Taiwan were the first to get started, a fact that makes South Korea's productivity growth after 1980 surprising. The second factor is the mix of the industries that are being installed. Productivity tends to increase more rapidly in capital-intensive than in labor-intensive industries, unless the latter are being modernized.

Some light on the South Korean performance is thrown by the data in Table 2.15. National income rose by 7.61 percent annually

Table 2.14
Indexes of Real Output in Manufacturing per Employee (1980 = 100)

	South Korea	Malaysia	Philippines	Taiwan	Thailand
1967	29.0	-	-	43.0	-
1970	40.0	96.2	102.0	61.8	70.4
1975	71.3	94.2	124.8	72.0	76.3
1980	100	100	100	100	100
1985	139.9	136.2 [a]	104.9	117.9	137.5
1986	159.2	-	111.1	126.3	139.7

Sources: World Bank, *World Tables* (Washington, 1989–1990); Republic of China, *Statistical Yearbook* (Taipei, 1989), Table 72.
[a]1983

Table 2.15
Sources of Economic Growth in Korea, 1963–1982 (average annual percentage rates)

National income	<u>7.61</u>
Total factor input	<u>4.89</u>
Labor:	<u>3.31</u>
Employment	2.18
Average hours worked	0.40
Age-sex composition	0.06
Education	0.39
Other	0.28
Capital	1.58

Source: Kim Kwang-suk and Park Joon-kyung, *Sources of Economic Growth in Korea, 1963–1982* (Seoul, Korea Development Institute, 1985), p. 61.

between 1963 and 1982. Factor inputs accounted for 64 percent of total growth, broken down into 43 percent for labor and 21 percent for capital inputs. The remaining 36 percent can be attributed to increases in the productivity of labor and capital. Most of the labor-input contribution came from increased employment.

Productivity is a powerful engine of development. With manufacturing labor productivity rising by 9 percent per annum in South Korea and by 6 percent in Taiwan over a 19-year period, it is not surprising that both have attained the status of newly industrialized countries. By way of contrast, Philippine productivity hardly changed.

To sum up, industrial growth in the five Asian countries was not constrained by lack of manpower. Their labor-force participation rates were high, both for men and women. Sufficient resources were allocated to education to provide necessary labor skills. Unemployment and underemployment were greatly reduced, if not eliminated, where the rate of growth was sufficiently high.

Labor absorption was greatest where labor productivity rose most rapidly. This might seem paradoxical, since an increase in labor productivity implies less need for labor. The explanation is that higher productivity of labor means greater capital intensity, which can result in rising output and profits which in turn, if a sufficient proportion is reinvested, can increase the demand for labor. The dynamism of the South Korean and Taiwanese economies owes a great deal to this sequence. We need only note that manufacturing output in South Korea was 17 times greater in 1988 than in 1968, and 12 times greater in Taiwan over the same period. Despite their high rates of productivity growth, by 1988 there were four times more manufacturing jobs in South Korea and almost that many more in Taiwan than there had been 20 years earlier.

NOTES

1. J. A. C. Mackie, "Economic Growth in the ASEAN Region," in Helen Hughes (editor), *Achieving Industrialization in East Asia* (Cambridge: Cambridge University Press, 1988), p. 300.

2. For a good discussion of this issue see Rosa Linda P. Tidalgo and Emmanuel F. Biguerra, *Philippine Employment in the 1970s* (Manila: Philippine Institute for Development Studies, 1982).

3. The participation rates in Tables 2.8 and 2.9 cannot be compared with those in Table 2.6. The latter represent the ratio of females in the labor force to the total female population, while the former show the proportion of women workers in the economically active population.

4. Harry Oshima, "Human Resources and Productivity Trends," in Shinichi Ichimura (editor), *Challenge of Asian Developing Countries* (Tokyo: Asia Productivity Organization, 1988), p. 94.

5. Tony Mitchell, *From a Developing to a Newly Industrialized Country: The Republic of Korea* (Geneva: International Labor Organization, 1988), p. 104.

6. It is reported that by 1990, some 600 Taiwan-born scientists and engineers who had been employed in the United States had returned to Taiwan. The engineers earned only about one-third to one-half their American salaries, but the attraction was the possibility of rapidly rising incomes in the many small high-technology firms in Taiwan. The *New York Times*, November 26, 1990, p. D1.

7. Manning Nash (editor), *Economic Performance in Malaysia* (New York: Paragon House, 1987), p. 60.

8. Jang-ho Kim, *Wages, Employment, and Income Distribution in South Korea, 1960–1983* (New Delhi: ARTEP, 1985), pp. 58–59.

9. U.S. Department of Labor, *Foreign Labor Trends: Taiwan* (Washington, 1987), p. 5.

10. The following discussion is based on International Labor Office, *Employment Issues and Policies for Thailand's Sixth Plan* (Geneva, 1985).

11. Malaysia, *Fifth Malaysian Plan, 1986–1990* (Kuala Lumpur, 1986), pp. 139–147.

12. Rene E. Ofreno and Esther P. Habana, *The Employment Crisis and the World Bank's Adjustment Program* (Quezon: Institute of Industrial Relations, 1987), pp. 73–74.

13. Philippines, Economic Development Authority, *Updated Philippine Development Plan, 1984–1987* (Manila, 1984), p. 23.

14. World Bank, *Philippines: A Framework for Economic Recovery* (Washington, 1987).

3

Industrial Relations

The creation of productive employment opportunities is only the first step in deploying a labor force. Qualified employees must be found, hired, trained, and provided with working conditions that stimulate effective performance. Procedures to determine pay, to deal with complaints, and to ensure positive attitudes toward work must be established. An industrial relations system that will help maximize output is needed.

When the present-day industrial nations first began their economic development, individual workers were recruited, assigned to jobs, and paid whatever the employer deemed appropriate. They worked long hours under what were often unpleasant and dangerous conditions. Trade unions were formed in the quest for higher wages and improved conditions. Collective bargaining replaced individual bargaining, and the strike weapon came to be used as part of it. This was an almost universal pattern among the wealthier nations of the world, although there were great variations in detail.

The newly developing countries are undergoing a similar evolution, although within a greatly compressed time frame. Some already had trade unions when they gained independence; others were encouraged to allow some form of collective bargaining by external pressures from foreign trade unions and by the force of emulation. The presence or absence of a previous colonial power is an important datum in this respect. The British influence in Malaysia and the American in the Philippines established a basis for trade unionism in those countries. This was not the case in independent Thailand or in Japanese-dominated Taiwan and Korea, where labor organization was not encouraged, even in the relatively few nonagricultural occupations where it might have been appropriate.

Whether trade unions and collective bargaining help or hinder economic development has been the subject of considerable debate. Those who hold a negative view argue that effective unions may secure wages that are higher than the marginal product of labor and reduce the investment resources essential to growth. Labor-intensive production, characteristic of the early stages of industrialization, may be frustrated if hours of work are too short and wages raised beyond internationally competitive levels. Work stoppages may impair the orderly scheduling of production. Trade unions may make it difficult to discharge unsuitable workers. In this scenario, collective bargaining may be appropriate when a sufficient degree of industrialization has been achieved, but not in the early stages of development.

The arguments for earlier employee organization stress what might be termed the productive function of trade unions rather than their role in furthering consumption. Collective agreements can serve as a disciplinary force by obliging union members to abide by their terms. In providing a means for redressing legitimate grievances, unions may help remove festering discontent that may lead to low productivity. Bringing some democracy into the workshop may help avert the violent outbursts that often follow repression.

All of our five Asian countries have seen the establishment of labor organizations, but they have varied greatly in form and function. Among the factors that have influenced their emergence have been the relative size of the industrial sector, the size of newly established enterprises, and an extremely important political factor—the extent and level of democracy. Military autocrats have not been inclined to look with favor on unions, while democratic governments have at least been obliged to tolerate them.

TRADE UNIONISM

At the present writing, of our five Asian countries, South Korea has the strongest labor movement, although this is of very recent origin. Prior to 1987, the trade unions were in a constant struggle to keep alive.

After the liberation of South Korea from Japanese rule, a newly formed communist-controlled labor federation was banned by the U.S. military authorities and a more conservative body, the Federation of Korean Trade Unions (FKTU), was substituted for it. A good many small local unions were established, and membership rose from 205,500 to 356,600 by April 1961. There was particularly rapid growth during 1960–1961, when the unions mounted hundreds of demonstrations in support of the short-lived Republic. The FKTU had increasingly become a satellite of the ruling Liberal party, but it was reorganized in 1960 in an effort to make it independent.

The military coup that put General Park in power in May, 1961, led to the Federation's dissolution, but it was reorganized a few months later. The structural model chosen was that of Germany; fourteen national unions along strictly industrial lines were organized. Membership rose slowly; the 1960 level was not regained until 1966. Then, under the impact of rapid industrialization, membership continued to climb, reaching the one-million mark in 1978.

But the FKTU and its affiliates were brought under the control of the government and served to moderate rather than advance local union demands. In the mid-1970s, the government turned over to the unions administration of the national medical insurance and pension systems and began to crack down on employer unfair-labor practices, but once again progress was stalled by the assassination of President Park and the formation of an antiunion government under Chun Doo Hwan. Increased emphasis was placed on enterprise-level local unions along Japanese lines, and the authority of the national unions diminished. Membership, which had fallen in 1980, regained the one-million mark in 1983, but stagnated during the next five years. The government allowed the unions to represent employees in grievance matters, but maintained close supervision over their economic activities. This led to the conclusion in a 1986 study prepared for the World Bank that "the influence of trade unions over the Korean labor market has . . . been very small."[1]

This phase of union status came to an end with the presidential election of 1987, which was won by Rho Tae Woo after a bitter three-party fight. His administration relinquished control over the unions and, for the first time in South Korean history, a genuinely independent labor movement emerged.

By the end of 1989, total membership in Korean unions was 1.83 million, constituting 22 percent of the organizable labor force. The FKTU is the largest of three labor factions, with 20 national affiliates and more than one million members. In opposition to it are the so-called democratic unions, consisting of unions formed after 1987 that refused to join the FKTU on the ground that the latter was tainted because of its earlier cooperation with the government. These unions set up a new federation, the National Council of Labor Unions, in January, 1990, and claimed a membership of 200,000. Shortly after the inauguration of the new body, its chairman was arrested for violation of a law prohibiting the creation of more than one union at each organizational level. A third segment consists of unions that are nominally affiliated with the FKTU but do not participate in its activities for political and personal reasons.[2]

The Labor Union Law, which governs the operation of trade unions, sets a maximum permissible-dues limit of 2 percent of earnings. The FKTU receives only 0.02 percent of the dues collected by its affiliates, and its national affiliates receive 0.07 percent. These amounts are not sufficient to sustain much in the way of organizational and other activities at supraenterprise levels.

The unions suffer from the additional handicap of being prohibited from supporting candidates for political office, a ban they are attempting to have repealed.[3]

To summarize, although trade unions have been in existence ever since the country was liberated from Japanese domination, they were under strict government control for most of these years and had little impact on the development process. Only since 1987 have they gained sufficient power to affect economic events. If this trend continues, South Korea may be the first of the newly industrializing Asian countries to have a modern labor movement.

The history of the Philippine labor movement is somewhat different from that of South Korea. It was relatively free of government control for many of the postwar years, but its effectiveness was limited by fragmentation into competing groups. Geographical dispersion of the labor force, ideological antagonisms, and the rival ambitions of leaders contributed to the frustration of efforts toward unity.

In the immediate postwar years, a labor federation controlled by the Communist party became the most important labor organization, but it was dissolved in 1951 and its leaders imprisoned. New organizations were formed and membership grew slowly. After the imposition of martial law in 1972, the Marcos regime attempted to bring about some consolidation by setting minimum standards for their compulsory registration as legitimate labor organizations, but this proved unsuccessful.

The restoration of political democracy in 1986 allowed for more freedom of action, but much of the renewed effort went into intense interunion rivalry. However, the unions have made moderate progress. It is estimated that there are about 2.4 million organized workers, 10.2 percent of the labor force. There are almost 4,000 registered local unions, double the number in 1985. The largest labor federation is the Trade Union Congress of the Philippines (TUCP) with 40 national affiliates. The Federation of Free Workers and the Lakas Manggagawa Labor Center are smaller organizations that have joined into a loose coalition with the TUCP. In opposition to these organizations is the May First Movement (KMU), which heads a smaller conglomerate called the Labor Advisory and Consultative Council.[4]

The TUCP and the KMU represent opposite poles of the labor movement. The former espouses cooperation with employers in the interest of development, for which it was denounced as a "yellow" union by the KMU, which calls for militant action to develop class consciousness among workers. KMU affiliates have mounted a number of strikes well out of proportion to their membership. Unions of their political orientation would not be allowed to exist in the other four Asian countries in our set.

As in the case of South Korea, much of the strength of the labor movement resides in local unions, many of which are not affiliated with any national unions, particularly in larger enterprises. Some of these unions have joined together in loose organizations, adding to the complexity of union structure.[5]

An interesting feature of the Philippine labor movement is the key leadership role played by lawyers, a not uncommon phenomenon in developing countries, where physicians also are often prominent in unions. In the Philippines, all disputes were referred to a government tribunal for resolution until 1953, and the unions became dependent on lawyers to represent them. For lawyers, this was a way to develop a practice and to secure a base for election to political office. But the danger was that economic demands were subordinated to political considerations.

Philippine trade-union history also illustrates another aspect of labor in developing economies. Given high unemployment, employers need not be overly concerned about unionization of their employees. Union bargaining power is low, particularly where interunion rivalry prevails. It may be that freedom from government domination is a necessary condition for the expansion of independent unionism, but the Philippine experience shows that it is not a sufficient condition.

The Malaysian labor movement has faced some handicaps that prevented it from reaching its full potential: racial divisions and strict government regulation. All new unions are required to report to the Registrar of Trade Unions, which may deny recognition if "there is already in existence a trade union in respect of the particular trade, occupation or industry, and if it is not in the interest of the workmen concerned that there be another trade union of a similar character." This has the virtue of preventing splintered unions as in the Philippines, but it has the vice of restricting unions to a single industry or company. General or multi-industrial unions are effectively barred.

The end of the Japanese occupation in 1945 led to a burst of union activity under the aegis of the Communist party. The communist purge undertaken by the British colonial authorities destroyed this abortive labor federation, whose officers were either arrested or fled to the jungle to join guerrillas. A new federation, the Malaysian Trade Union Congress (MTUC) replaced it. Progress was slow until the onset of industrialization during the 1960s. By 1968, some 300,000 employees had been organized, but growth was interrupted by the race riots of 1969 and the subsequent state of emergency. Upward movement resumed with the restoration of normalcy and, by 1983, total membership reached 568,000. After several years of stagnation, membership rose once again and was up to 617,000 by the end of 1988.

The MTUC remains the country's dominant labor federation with 300,000 members and 142 affiliated unions. There is also the Congress of Unions of Employees in the Public and Civil Service with 110,000 members. A number of large national unions, including those in the petroleum industry, banking, and commerce remain independent.

An interesting feature of Malaysian unionism is the strength of organization among workers on the large rubber plantations. The National Union of Plantation Workers, with 83,000 members, is the largest in the country. It has a great deal of prestige both in Malaysia and abroad, due to a considerable extent to the reputation of one of its founders—P. P. Narayanan, who has not only been its secretary-general for more than two decades but is also in his fourth term as president of the International Confederation of Free Trade

Unions, the dominant international body of labor. P. P., as he is widely known, is probably the most prominent labor leader in all the developing nations.

Given its long history and relative stability, it is surprising to find that the Malaysian labor movement has been able to organize only 10 percent of the nonagricultural labor force, including the plantation workers. One reason is that manufacturing and service enterprises are predominantly small and difficult to organize. There is also the fact that a quarter of the plantation labor force consists of temporary workers on term contracts who do not join the union. The labor movement has been weakened in recent years by the growth of company unions, particularly in the public sector, with the encouragement of the Prime Minister, who is an advocate of the Japanese model of enterprise-level unions. These unions, unaffiliated with the MTUC, had one-third of all union members in 1988.[6]

Thai unions have had a much harder time, faced as they were with a very large agricultural sector and the late inception of industrialization. As in the other countries, the first postwar unions were initiated by communists, drawn primarily from the country's Chinese minority. They were dissolved in 1952 and many of their leaders imprisoned. To counteract their influence, the Thai National Trade Union Congress (TNTUC) was formed with the assistance of the Prime Minister. A number of national trade unions also came into being, generally under the patronage of high government officials. At its peak the TNTUC enrolled 30,000 workers, but it led a hazardous existence.

The government that attained power by a coup in 1958 destroyed even this modest beginning of a labor movement and inaugurated what one writer has called the dark ages of Thai labor. "The fourteen-year period between 1958 and 1972 was one in which formal labor organization did not exist."[7] There were a few strikes but they were of short duration and settled by the government.

With the overthrow of the military government in 1973 and the installation of a democratic regime, which lasted for three years before being replaced once again by the military, there was a burst of worker activism. In 1972 there were 34 strikes involving 7,800 workers; in the following year, there were 500 strikes and 178,000 strikers. "The lid was off; demonstrations were in vogue; and dissatisfied economic groups were quick to give vent to their frustrations. . . . Demonstrations were truly at the grassroots level, occurring in response to every conceivable complaint."[8] Some 150 local unions were formed, though at the national level there was a split between militant and more conservative leaders.

Fortunately for labor, the generals who took over in 1976 were not as repressive as their predecessors. Responding to foreign pressure, the government allowed the unions more freedom than they had enjoyed in the past. Membership rose from 50,000 in 1975 to 217,000 in 1983 and reached 309,000 by 1989. Nevertheless, with only 3 percent of the industrial labor force organized, Thailand has the lowest level of unionization among our five Asian countries. To make matters worse, the Thai labor movement is split into five rival centers, and even these are ridden by internal factions.

A unique aspect of Thai unionism is the relative strength of the public sector organizations, which among them account for half of total union membership, whose main concern is to prevent privatization of such state enterprises as the airlines and the telephone system. "Private sector organization [has] progressed only marginally, due to a number of legal and cultural factors conspiring against further organization in private firms, such as ineffective legal bars to unfair dismissal and traditionally paternalistic relations between employer and employee."[9]

An ominous note was interjected into the Thai labor scene in March, 1991, when the new military leaders announced that they were considering a ban on unions in the nationalized industries, presumably for the purpose of eliminating potential political opposition. This was to be effected by amending the Labor Relations Act of 1975 to deprive public sector employees of the right to organize or strike. If this plan were to be carried out, it would decimate the Thai labor movement.

Turning finally to Taiwan, the Chinese Federation of Labor (CFL), which had moved with Chiang Kai-shek from the mainland in 1950, was almost moribund until 1975. Its national union affiliates existed, but did little in the way of collective bargaining. The unions were reactivated in 1976 and for the first time, Taiwan had a functioning labor movement. Pressure from the International Confederation of Free Trade Unions and from the AFL-CIO contributed to this development.

However, the unions operated under severe restrictions. They were forbidden to call strikes, and their ability to bargain on wages was limited. Half of their officers were members of the Kuomintang, until recently Taiwan's only political party, and some were members of the national legislature. However, even in these early years, the unions were not powerless. They entered into collective agreements with management on a variety of issues, excluding wages, and they handled grievances. Managers discovered that labor adjustments went more smoothly if their local unions were consulted, but management domination was an ever present danger.[10]

Despite these handicaps, the unions were able to increase their membership and authority. Membership rose from 765,000 in 1975 to 1.87 million in 1987. Some quasiunions called "friendship associations" also emerged because of growing worker dissatisfaction with the formal unions.

Things changed drastically in 1987, when the martial law regimen that had been in effect since 1950 was lifted. At the end of 1989 there were 3,500 local unions in Taiwan with a membership of 2.53 million. This represented 30.5 percent of all employees. Unions that organized service workers—barbers, cab drivers, food vendors—grew most rapidly. However, a string of lost strikes resulted in some loss of momentum for the labor movement after 1989, particularly in the large firms.

None of this means that unions are free to organize and operate as they please. Under the 1975 Labor Union Law, trade union structure must conform to certain criteria. Craft and industrial local unions are based on the individual enterprise and can federate only at the district level, thus curbing the creation of national industrial unions. Only unions in government enterprises with more than seven branches are permitted to form national organizations and operate on a country-wide basis.

Strikes became legal in 1988 for the first time with the enactment of labor disputes legislation, although the government retained the authority to declare them illegal under certain circumstances. A rash of work stoppages took place, involving the railroads, busses, postal service, gas stations, and docks, and the authorities allowed them to proceed, although most were illegal, "partly because they recognized the legitimacy of some of the workers' demands but most importantly because they feared the political backlash of heavy-handed action."[11]

Some strikes in private enterprises were treated with less leniency. A strike in 1989 at the Far Eastern Textile Company had been approved by a two-thirds vote of the employees, as required by law, but it was declared illegal because the union had not received the necessary permit from the local government. There was some violence on the picket line, and several union activists were arrested.[12] Employers have taken a hard line in other strikes, and the government has generally backed them up. The prevalence of small enterprises also makes it more difficult for unions to organize and operate effectively.

Several factors contributed to the recent rise of unionism in Taiwan. On the economic side, the growing shortage of domestic labor reduced the freedom of employers to act without heed to the demands of their employees. Of greater importance was the expansion of political democracy. Opposition parties have been permitted to operate openly and to support candidates in national and local elections. The opposition groups won 41 percent of the votes at the 1989 elections. The present president of Taiwan, Lee Teng-hui, is the first person holding that office to have been born in Taiwan, marking the beginning of the end of political domination by emigres from the mainland. Even if the Kuomintang retains its majority, a return to pre-1987 conditions does not appear to be in the cards. Taiwan has entered the ranks of the developed nations, and it cannot afford to reinstate the repressive conditions that marked its dash from Asian backwardness to economic maturity. To quote a U.S. Government publication: "labor activism may be expected to continue to grow. Taiwan's labor movement, like Taiwan's political structure, has recently been liberated by the lifting of martial law. It is groping for a new equilibrium at which economic development, management concerns, and labor demands can be reconciled."[13]

Reviewing the history of trade unionism in the five Asian countries, there are some interesting regularities, despite great differences in background. In the immediate postwar period, unions were initiated by political groups seeking a base of support. As industry expanded, so did the unions, the pace of expansion depending on a combination of economic and political events. All five countries ended up with viable labor movements, though their coverage depended largely on the nature of the industrial structure in which they operated. It is not surprising that union density is highest in South Korea and Taiwan, and lowest in Thailand. A tendency toward the splitting of each of the labor movements into rival organizations limits their power, and until they achieve some degree of unity their ability to bargain effectively will remain circumscribed. It might be worth noting that the Japanese labor movement, which had a somewhat similar history to those of the five Asian countries, and which was seriously divided, did not manage to achieve unity until 1989.

COLLECTIVE BARGAINING

Once trade unions are in place, a system of bargaining must be established. The process may be bilateral, or the government may be involved as a third party. Rules for settling impasses are essential, involving mediation or arbitration. The latter may be voluntary or compulsory. Separate procedures for new contracts or for disputes over existing contracts may be specified. The system may be developed by management and unions alone, but in developing countries the government almost always plays a leading role in initiating procedures and elaborating them when some experience is gained.

Then there is the question of strikes. Each side must have the option of saying no. To have genuine bargaining, the employer should have the right to refuse what he regards as importunate demands, while unions should be able to withhold the services of their members in the pursuit of what they consider legitimate demands. If a union cannot call a strike, it either has little bargaining power or it must rely on the political process to achieve its goals, and thus become dependent on government. The hallmark of an independent union is one that has the legal right to strike and exercises it on occasion. A union that never calls a strike may be suspected of being under the domination of the employer or of the government.

Industrial relations in South Korea have been subjected to strict government regulation. The basic regulations are embodied in the Labor Union Law and the Labor Disputes Adjustment Law, both originally enacted in 1953 and amended several times since. The former specifies in some detail the rules covering the internal governance of trade unions as well as setting forth employer unfair-labor practices. Among the latter are discharge for union membership, refusal to sign a collective agreement, and domination of a union. Complaints may be lodged with the government Labor Relations Committee and its regional affiliates, which can levy penalties for violation.

The unfair-labor practices were modeled on U.S. labor legislation and were designed to protect union organization, but "there has been a gap between written labor law and actual practice. Management often ignored legal protections given to labor with little threat of government enforcement."[14] Surveillance was tightened after 1986; one piece of evidence is that the number of unfair-labor charges filed rose from 511 in 1986 to 1771 in 1987, suggesting that unions had greater confidence in the possibility of redress.

Under the Labor Disputes Adjustment Law, if an employer and union cannot reach agreement and a work stoppage is imminent, the parties are required to notify the Labor Relations Committee at least 10 days before the stoppage is to begin in the private sector and 15 days in the state sector. The committee may appoint a conciliator, and if he cannot secure agreement, a tripartite mediation board is set up. If this fails, the parties are free to stop work.

If an industry is designated as vital to the public welfare, there is a mandatory cooling-off period of 30 days, and if no agreement is reached within that period, compulsory arbitration may be imposed. Among the vital industries are transportation and communications, utilities, health, and banking, as well as industries owned or run by the central or municipal governments. The unions have not been happy with this system, but have had to live with it. Police have been used to break illegal strikes in Poongsan Metal, a munitions producer, the Seoul subway system, and Hyundai Heavy Industries, one of the country's largest enterprises.[15]

These are the legal regulations, but actual events often take a different course. "Many negotiations tend to lead to strikes before an impasse is reached. In many cases, workers use other industrial actions, such as sit-ins, to put pressure on management to negotiate seriously. The pattern of 'industrial actions first, negotiations later' has become popular, especially at the time of establishing a new union."[16]

An interesting union demand is that workers should be paid for time lost during a strike, arguing that since unions have little in the way of strike funds, this is the only way to equalize bargaining power. Although employers and the government are opposed to this practice, it is estimated that full or partial payments were made subsequent to 80 percent of the strikes that took place in 1989.[17] But the government began to clamp down on this practice by urging industry to adopt a policy of "no work, no pay" and ruling that demands for strike pay were not the basis for legal strikes.

The year 1987 marked a major change in South Korean labor relations. In 1986, 276 disputes were notified to labor relations commissions; in 1987 there were 3,749. The number dropped in 1988, but the strike duration rate rose from 5 days to 12 days, and to 18 days in 1989. There was a growing tendency toward violence on both sides, sometimes because of divisions among workers into radical and conservative factions. Union leaders charged that companies were hiring thugs to assault organizers and strikers, while police were used to oust sit-down strikers and quell disturbances. An aide to President Roh was quoted as saying that "the labor situation is one of our thorniest problems. Both the workers and businessmen aren't used to these problems, and neither is the Government."[18]

An effort had been made to sidetrack the unions by mandating the creation of labor-management councils at the enterprise level, consisting of an equal representation of workers and management to deal with grievances and to spur productivity. Their success in settling grievances was mixed. In nonunion firms they were dominated by the employer, while in organized firms union officials were generally chosen as employee representatives, providing another forum for confrontation. The government has also been attempting to reconcile the positions of the various interest groups through a tripartite National Wage Mediation Committee.

During its years of rapid growth, South Korea failed to develop an adequate system of collective bargaining and began paying the price when authoritarian government control was ended in 1987. It has been estimated that production lost due to labor disputes amounted to between 5 and 6 billion dollars in 1989. A World Bank study written in 1986, before the labor explosion, concluded that "although bargaining in some sense is carried on, the actual determination of wages for each occupational group is usually done unilaterally by the employer, subject only to workers' pressure and to informal discussion with branch officials." The report also noted that there were few legal sanctions for violation of contracts even where they existed.[19] It should come as no surprise that econometric studies from this period found no independent union effect on wages. Market forces determined both the level and structure of wages.

This conclusion would not hold after 1987. Manufacturing wages rose by almost 20 percent in 1988 and by the same amount in 1989. Would it have been better strategy to allow the unions more power earlier, even at the expense of higher wage levels, and avoided the sharp wage burst that followed the years of repression? It can be argued that double digit growth rates would have been impossible with higher wages. On the other hand, the halving of GNP growth from 1988 to 1989, to which labor strife contributed, might have been avoided. The wage increases of 1988 and 1989 were far out of line with both labor productivity and consumer prices. The South Korean experience poses a question that developing countries have to face sooner or later, if they are to develop.

The Philippines have had no lack of labor legislation. The Industrial Peace Act of 1953 underwent many revisions which went to make up the 1974 Labor Code. Prior to that year, workers and unions had recourse only to the courts to redress grievances, typically a lengthy process that could take as long as ten years. The Code established a National Labor Relations Commission under the Department of Labor to hear appeals from arbitrators named in collective agreements. The Minister of Labor was named commission chairman, and the president himself was empowered to intervene if he deemed it appropriate. The right to organize and bargain collectively was guaranteed, although government and nonprofit agencies were not covered by the guarantee. Unions were required to register with a government body, and they had the exclusive right to represent employees in an appropriate bargaining unit. Collective agreements were to be for a minimum of three years.

Modeled after legislation in the United States, the 1974 code seemed to establish the framework for fruitful collective bargaining. The fly in the ointment was in the provisions relating to strikes. They were prohibited in "vital" industries as determined by the government. A list of such industries promulgated in 1975 omitted few sectors of the economy so that, in effect, labor disputes were subject to compulsory arbitration.

Work stoppages continued, but at a low level and of short duration. When Marcos ended martial law in 1981, he modified the 1974 Labor Code by substituting "national interest" for "vital industries" as the criterion for prohibiting strikes, opening the door a bit. The reaction was a surge of strikes in 1981, mostly to protest employer unfair-labor practices. The government clamped down, and a number of union leaders were jailed.

Unrest continued, however, culminating in a wave of strikes with the election of Corazon Aquino to the presidency in 1986. This was similar to what took place in South Korea a year later, though against a background of economic recession rather than growth and despite heavy unemployment. The government warned against illegal strikes and forcibly removed barricades put up by picketers. "These developments adversely affected the strike-prone leftist unions whose leaders appeared to be more interested in sabotaging the economy and intimidating business and government than in securing benefits for their members."[20]

Things began to improve with the adoption of a new constitution that guaranteed the right to organize, bargain collectively, and strike, and the enactment in 1989 of legislation that provided the framework for an orderly system of industrial relations. Sponsored by Senator Ernesto Herrera, who was secretary-general of the Philippine Trade Union Congress, the law called for wider use of voluntary arbitration and converted the National Labor Relations Commission into a tripartite body independent of the Labor Department. It restricted the right of the Minister of Labor to intervene in strikes only to those "indispensable" to the national interest; it legalized strikes in government and nonprofit enterprises; it provided that union officers were to be directly elected for five-year terms; and it gave supervisory personnel the right to organize.

The most important recent policy measure adopted by the government was the promotion of the tripartite Industrial Peace Accord of 1990, joined by all unions except the radical KMU. It commits the parties to peaceful voluntary modes of dispute settlement. No-strike clauses are recommended for collective agreements, but they are not required. In exchange for the peace pledge on the part of the unions, the government agreed to consider a nonwage package advocated by the unions and to provide funds for the operation of regional wage boards.[21]

It is too soon to tell whether the new legislation will bring about a permanent improvement in Philippine industrial relations. Much depends on political developments, particularly because the labor movement is split along ideological lines. The first half of 1990 saw a sharp increase in strikes compared with the similar period in 1989. Unions of government employees displayed particular militancy.

Unsatisfactory labor relations have contributed to lagging economic development in the Philippines, primarily by discouraging investment by both domestic and foreign entrepreneurs. However, the unions appear to have had little effect on wages, at least until recently. Only since 1986 have money wages begun to outstrip consumer prices, and a 39 percent increase in the minimum wage in 1989 was largely due to union pressure. Philippine wages would have been low enough to make manufacturing internationally competitive if industry had not been sheltered by the protectionist policies followed by the various governments.

Malaysia has the best-developed industrial-relations system of the five countries. This is not to say that a free, untrammeled labor market has been in effect. The government maintained strong control over the conduct of collective bargaining, and the power of the unions was kept within strict bounds. The basic legislation governing the system are the Industrial Relations Acts of 1977 and 1980. The first of these laws set the framework for collective bargaining; the second gave the government greater authority to deal with disruptive strikes.

Enterprise-level collective bargaining is the norm. Either the employer or the union may request the Industrial Relations Department of the Ministry of Labor to send in conciliators if the parties are not able to reach agreement on their own. Most disputes, whether over rights or interests, are resolved at this level. If conciliation fails, the Minister of Labor may refer the case to an Industrial Court for final resolution. A majority of the cases referred involve contract interpretation and compliance. In the event that the ministry decides to refer the case, the union is barred from striking, that is, it must accept compulsory arbitration. The court is tripartite, the partisan members being nominated by the MTUC and the Malayan Employers Federation.

Legislation enacted in 1988 changed the bargaining rules in several details but did not alter the fundamental structure. Under the previous law, union representation claims were determined by checking union registration lists against payrolls. Secret ballots were added as an additional means of determining representation claims. Industrial court awards were made enforcible by the regular courts, replacing the previous practice of going to the police to secure compliance.

A major concern of the government has been to minimize industrial strife, and it has succeeded in this thanks to its ability to invoke compulsory arbitration of disputes. There were only nine strikes involving 2,129 workers in 1988, a majority of them on the plantations. Some 1,234 disputes were notified to the Ministry of Labor, of which 84 were referred to the Industrial Court. In 1987, the court decided 66 cases involving new contracts. As further evidence of the government's reluctance to countenance anything that might interfere with investment, it has prohibited union negotiation of such issues as promotion, transfer, new hiring, assignment of duties, dismissal, and reinstatement, with firms that have been designated as "pioneers," which also means tax-free status for a normal period of five years with the possibility of renewal.[22]

These regulations do not add up to authoritarian rule over industrial relations. The unions are not creatures of the government. They have defended the interests of their members in a number of areas of employment. They have participated actively in the proceedings of the Industrial Court. How much influence they have had on wages can only be determined by a careful analysis of the court's awards. The probability is that market forces plus government policy have been the decisive factors in wage determination.

Thailand was late in setting up a system of industrial relations, but one has emerged, at least in terms of appropriate legislation.

Prior to 1975 there were statutes on the books, but little in the way of trade unionism or collective bargaining. The breakthrough came with the enactment of the Labor Relations Act of 1975, which established the right to employees to organize and provided some protection for unions engaged in collective bargaining. It set up a system of conciliation and arbitration and delineated the sectors of the economy in which strikes were permitted.

Unorganized employees can initiate a demand for a collective agreement if at least 15 percent of the total number of employees in an enterprise sponsor it, while unions representing at least 20 percent of the employees can also take such action. The employer has three days to respond, followed by negotiations. If an agreement is reached, it must be reduced to writing and displayed for 30 days at a public place in the enterprise, as well as registered with the Department of Labor.

Should negotiations end in an impasse, a government conciliator is called in, and he has five days to bring about a resolution of the dispute. If he fails, the parties may agree to voluntary arbitration, or else initiate a work stoppage. Strikes are prohibited in public utilities, hospitals, public enterprises, and transportation facilities; and in such other enterprises as the Minister of the Interior deems essential to the economy or public order, or that will result in hardship to the public or endanger national security. In such cases the minister may send the dispute to final adjudication by the Labor Relations Commission, a tripartite public body.

There were a great many strikes during the brief period of civilian rule from 1973 to 1976. During the following five years strikes were banned by the military government, though a few did occur. The strike ban was removed in 1981, but work stoppages remained small in number and duration due to the weakness of the unions and the fact that more than half of all union members were employed in the state sector, where strikes were strictly forbidden.[23]

Labor courts were created in 1979 to hear and decide disputes over contracts. The courts may attempt conciliation, but if that fails they make final decisions, taking into consideration working and living conditions, hardship to the employees, the level of wages or other rights and benefits of the employees doing the same type of work, the status of the business of the employer, and general economic and social conditions.

The government has encouraged labor-management cooperation at the enterprise level to supplement collective bargaining. The Labor Relations Act of 1975 provided for the establishment of employees' committees either by polling the employees or by union designation. These committees are supposed to meet with employers at least once every three months to discuss employee welfare, work regulations, and employee complaints. The committees are not popular with the unions, which have generally taken the position that they are employer dominated and serve mainly to rubber stamp management policies.

Prior to the 1988 elections, a number of strikes took place in state enterprises, including one that tied up the railway system. The outgoing Prem administration, instead of resorting to breaking the strikes by arresting the leaders, agreed to the union demands. The incoming Chatichai administration, the first to be elected in more than a decade, sought closer relations with the unions and "operated in an improved spirit of openness and accessibility which initially won friends in the labor movement."[24] But the unions soon became annoyed by the policies followed by the government, particularly its attempt to privatize the railroads, utilities, and telephone systems, a move prompted by the need to raise private capital for these enterprises.

Thailand has finally adopted a labor relations system that is consistent with its graduation into the ranks of the newly industrialized countries. What still remains to be accomplished on the labor side is consolidation of the competing labor centers into a movement that can secure for workers a more adequate share of the fruits of economic growth. The government will have to resolve the problem of bargaining rights for employees in the large public sector. The opposition of the unions to privatization suggests that the greater security of employment in public enterprises outweighs the still limited freedom to bargain in the private sector.

Turning to Taiwan, the principal observation to be made is that its system of industrial relations is of very recent vintage. Prior to 1987, there was little collective bargaining in the Western sense, and unions did not have the right to strike. Some firms engaged in informal discussions with local unions on a variety of issues in the belief that this contributed to employee morale. All firms were required to set up bipartite factory councils to discuss problems of plant welfare, safety and health measures, and pending personnel actions. The councils were supposed to meet monthly, but many did not meet that frequently—and some were not established at all.

As already noted, the labor scene changed abruptly with the lifting of martial law in 1987. Local mediation and arbitration commissions failed to curb strikes, but the government hoped that the appointment of a national mediation agency would lead the parties to settle their disputes peacefully. In recognition of the need for developing a viable system of collective bargaining, the Labor Department, which had been part of the Ministry of the Interior, was upgraded to a Council of Labor Affairs under the direct jurisdiction of the cabinet. Thus far, Taiwan has succeeded in avoiding the kind of explosive labor market that occurred in South Korea, but it is still too early to foresee what kind of a system of industrial relations will eventually emerge.

SUMMARY

Table 3.1 contains data on strike activity in the form of the ratio between work days lost due to labor disputes and nonagricultural employment. (Taiwan does not publish data on labor disputes). Comparisons between the countries must be made with caution because of the effect of industrial structure on both parts of the ratio, including services versus manufacturing and enterprise size. A salient example is provided by Malaysia; it is the only country in which agriculture accounted for a large proportion of strikes because of the prevalence of large rubber plantations that are industrial in nature.

Table 3.1
Working Days Lost Due to Strikes or Lockouts as a Percentage of Paid Employment in Nonagricultural Activities, 1978–1989

	South Korea	Malaysia[a]	Philippines	Thailand
1978	0.16	1.48	1.96	0.14
1979	0.19	1.49	1.97	0.51
1980	0.68	0.35	1.27	0.08
1981	0.34	0.63	9.21	2.32
1982	0.12	0.28	0.02	1.40
1983	0.09	0.21	7.01	0.65
1984	0.19	0.30	19.74	2.18
1985	0.57	0.92	24.00	0.15
1986	0.61	0.47	54.62	1.72
1987	54.38	0.28	17.57	-
1988	40.05	-	-	-
1989	61.33	-	-	-

Source: International Labor Office, *Yearbook of Labor Statistics* (Geneva, 1990).
[a]These figures are overstated because the strikes were predominantly in agriculture. In 1987, for example, 70 percent of strike days lost were in agriculture.

Nevertheless, the data do provide a useful supplement to the information provided above. South Korea was remarkably strike free from 1978 to 1986, but during the subsequent years it surpassed the other countries in the incidence of labor controversy. The earlier record was a function of weak unions operating under strict government control. Malaysia also experienced relatively few disputes, since unions were not strong and a well-developed system of bargaining was available to the unions. The Thai strike curve displays greater volatility, with occasional outbursts alternating with periods of almost no activity. In the Philippines, when Marcos kept the lid on worker discontent, strike activity was low (except for 1981), but when martial law ended the strike curve took a sharp upward turn and reached levels unmatched by the other countries apart from South Korea.

In attempting to assess the relationship between trade unionism, collective bargaining, and economic growth, it is not possible to determine cause and effect with precision. In any econometric model, the labor-relations variables would be overshadowed by other variables. However, the data do suggest some rough trends worth noting.

Economic development tends to increase the propensity of workers to organize into trade unions because of their greater number and larger concentrations, as well as their political influence. Even dictatorial governments eventually yield to domestic and external pressures by allowing trade unions to play an expanding role in determining conditions of employment. The estimated densities of trade unionism (union membership as a proportion of the organizable labor force) in 1988 was as follows:[25]

South Korea	22.0	percent
Malaysia	10.1	percent
Philippines	10.0	percent
Taiwan	27.1	percent
Thailand	2.8	percent

These figures are far from precise, and they are not necessarily correlated with union power, but given the low state of unionism at the onset of industrialization they do indicate that labor organization accompanies economic development. It is no accident that the most advanced countries in our set had the highest union density rates and the most recent industrializer, Thailand, the lowest.

The reverse effect—the impact of trade unions on economic development—is not as clear. For most of the period under review unions were too weak to exercise much, if any, influence on wages. The exceptions are of very recent origin. The labor market turmoil that began in South Korea in 1987 does appear to have had an adverse impact on economic growth, and there is concern in Taiwan lest the South Korean model be followed. Trade unions cannot be blamed for the poor record of development in the Philippines, but longstanding, guerrilla warfare on the labor front compounded the difficulties of achieving steady growth.

Workers in increasing numbers formed unions despite strong employer resistance and government indifference, at best. They were motivated not only by the desire for higher wages, but also for the protection that unions afforded against arbitrary employment policies and unreasonable working conditions. All the countries had established formal mechanisms for mounting appeals against violation of employee legal or contract rights, and in most cases it would have been the unions that carried the burden of prosecuting the appeals. The alacrity with which workers organized when political changes conferred legitimacy on unions suggests that there were grievances that had been bottled up, and that venting them may contribute to raising the morale of the labor force in the long run.

To respond to the question raised at the beginning of this chapter, it would not be easy to sustain the proposition that collective bargaining hindered economic development in the five Asian countries on the basis of experience to date. Recent events may require this conclusion to be reexamined. Rates of growth are slowing, unions are gaining strength, and after a few years it may be possible to isolate the union effects and to explore the relationships with the same analytical tools employed in the analysis of similar phenomena in the industrialized world.

NOTES

1. Ray Richardson and Byung Whan Kim, *The Structure of Labor Markets in LDCs: Overview of South Korea 1953–1984* (Washington, World Bank Discussion Paper, 1986), p. 5.

2. U.S. Department of Labor, *Foreign Labor Trends: Korea* (Washington: GPO, 1989–1990), p. 4.

3. Taigi Kim, *The Political Economy of Industrial Relations in Korea* (Seoul: Korea Labor Institute, 1989), pp. 26–30.

4. U.S. Department of Labor, *Foreign Labor Trends: Philippines* (Washington: GPO, 1989–1990), pp. 9–10.

5. Ibbara A. Malonzo, "Trade Unions as Participatory Agents in the Philippine Industrial Relations System," *Philippine Journal of Industrial Relations*, nos. 1–2 (1985): pp. 68–76.

6. Basu Sharma, *Aspects of Industrial Relations in ASEAN* (Singapore: Institute of Southeast Asian Studies, 1985), pp. 49–55; U.S. Department of Labor, *Foreign Labor Trends: Malaysia* (Washington: GPO, 1988–1989), pp. 10–14.

7. Bevars D. Mabry, *The Development of Labor Institutions in Thailand* (Ithaca: Cornell University, Department of Asian Studies, 1979), p. 49.

8. Ibid., p. 59.

9. U.S. Department of Labor, *Foreign Labor Trends: Thailand* (Washington: GPO, 1990), p. 3.

10. See Walter Galenson, *Economic Growth and Structural Change in Taiwan* (Ithaca: Cornell University Press, 1979), pp. 425–32.

11. U.S. Department of Labor, *Foreign Labor Trends: Taiwan* (Washington: GPO, 1988–1989), p. 6.

12. Irene Yeung, "Labor Gets Organized," *Free China Review* (October, 1990): p. 31.

13. U.S. Department of Labor, *Foreign Labor Trends: Taiwan* (Washington: GPO, 1988–1989), p. 11.

14. U.S. Department of Labor, *Foreign Labor Trends: Korea* (Washington: GPO, 1988–1989), p. 4.

15. U.S. Department of Labor, *Foreign Labor Trends: Korea* (Washington: GPO, 1989–90), p. 5.

16. Taigi Kim, *The Political Economy of Industrial Relations*, p. 34.

17. Ibid.

18. The *New York Times*, June 10, 1989.

19. Ray Richardson and Byung Whan Kim, *Adjustments to Policy Changes: the Case of Korea*, Report No. DRD 239 (Washington: World Bank, October 1986), p. 14.

20. U.S. Department of Labor, *Foreign Labor Trends: Philippines* (Washington: GPO, 1987), p. 8.

21. U.S. Department of Labor, *Foreign Labor Trends: Philippines* (Washington: GPO, 1989–1990), pp. 8–9.

22. See Basu Sharma, *Aspects of Industrial Relations in ASEAN*, pp. 49–55; U.S. Department of Labor, *Foreign Labor Trends: Malaysia* (Washington: GPO, 1987–1988 and 1988–1989).

23. See A.M.A.H. Siddiqui (editor), *Labor Administration Profile on Thailand* (Bangkok: International Labor Office, 1988); Chira Hongladarom (editor), *Comparative Labor and Management: Japan and Thailand* (Bangkok: Thamasart University Press, 1983).

24. U.S. Department of Labor, *Foreign Labor Trends: Thailand* (Washington: GPO, 1990), p. 2.

25. The data are from various issues of U.S. Department of Labor, *Foreign Labor Trends*.

4

Wages and Hours

Economic theory tells us that if earnings are determined by market forces, the rate at which they rise should be consonant with the increase in the marginal productivity of labor. This would tend to be slow in the early, labor-intensive stage of development and quicken as the supply of labor begins to dry up and capital intensity takes over.

However, markets are far from free in developing countries, with the result that the theoretical expectations are not always realized. As has already been noted, government intervention in the labor market is the rule rather than the exception. Wages may be held down despite rising productivity, or raised beyond productivity if political expediency requires it. The absence of effective trade unions facilitates government policy operation. Jobs in the modern sector, particularly in manufacturing, are very desirable in the absence of alternative opportunities available to workers seeking employment, with the result that it is not until the surplus labor pools in the agricultural and traditional sectors are drained that employers find it necessary to raise wages in order to attract and hold sufficient labor. Even then, wages may be held down artificially by government decree, with the result that when controls are relaxed, corrective upward adjustment of wages may come in a jump. The recent experience of Singapore provides a good example.

All of this applies to real rather than nominal wages. To assuage employee discontent, money wages may be permitted to rise without regard to productivity with the result that costs and prices also increase. There may be a tradeoff between labor peace and inflation; worker demands may be satisfied by putting more money in their pay envelopes, but the efficiency costs of inflation can be high. Moreover, the money illusion will eventually vanish, and then the problem of cutting the wage-price spiral remains.

Three of the five Asian countries have been relatively successful in restraining inflation, as the data in Table 4.1 show. Inflation was a persistent problem in South Korea until 1982. This appears to have been due to a combination of forced investment in the face of a low propensity to save and to the impact of important raw material prices, oil in particular. The Philippines have had a chronic inflation problem that has been variously ascribed to a persistent trade imbalance that necessitated foreign borrowing, heavy investment in unproductive enterprises, and the maintenance of private consumption at the expense of savings. Despite the depression that the Philippines suffered during the first half of the 1980s, prices

Table 4.1
Average Annual Rates of Price Inflation, 1965–1988 (percent)

	1965-1980	1980-1988
South Korea	18.7	5.0
Malaysia	4.9	1.3
Philippines	11.7	15.6
Taiwan	8.4	2.7
Thailand	6.3	3.1

Sources: World Bank, *World Development Report* (Washington, 1988 and 1990); Republic of China, *Taiwan Statistical Data Book* (Taipei, 1988).

continued to rise rapidly. In 1989, the consumer price index rose
by 10.6 percent.

Changes in real wages during the 1980s—abstracting from price
inflation—appear in Tables 4.2 and 4.3. Both tables are restricted
to manufacturing. The data in Table 4.2 are compiled by the
International Labor Office (ILO) from reports submitted to it by
member nations and are published annually in its statistical yearbooks. The relevant data for Malaysia do not appear in this source,
nor in the country's own publications. Statistics for Taiwan are not
carried in any of the international organization yearbooks, but the
data that appear in this table are available from its domestic
publications.

Another set of manufacturing earnings statistics, this one including Malaysia, emanate from a World Bank publication, and are
shown in Table 4.3. There are some discrepancies between the two
sets. The World Bank data show Philippine real wages declining
from 1975 to 1980, while the ILO set shows an increase. One of the

Table 4.2
Indexes of Real Wages in Manufacturing, 1970–1989 (1980 = 100)

	South Korea	Philippines	Taiwan	Thailand
1970	48.7	-	53.6	-
1975	58.0	91.7[a]	55.2	96.0
1980	100	100	100	100
1981	99.0	99.6	102.1	97.1
1982	105.9	100.6	108.6	104.2
1983	110.9	106.0	114.0	98.5
1984	121.5	91.9	136.6	172.8
1985	130.4	89.4	129.4	181.2
1986	139.3	99.8	141.5	159.2
1987	150.6	-	154.3	-
1988	167.6	-	168.7	-
1989	198.2	-	176.2	-

Sources: International Labor Office, *Yearbook of Labor Statistics* (Geneva, 1990);
    Republic of China, *Yearbook of Labor Statistics* (Taipei, 1989).
[a]1976

Table 4.3
Indexes of Real Earnings per Employee in Manufacturing, 1970–1986
(1980 = 100)

	South Korea	Malaysia	Philippines	Thailand
1970	43.3	83.7	151.4	83.1
1975	57.1	78.3	122.1	87.8
1980	100	100	100	100
1981	98.3	102.1	102.5	104.7
1982	102.8	111.2	104.4	118.9
1983	109.0	119.1	127.5	126.4
1984	119.0	125.0	110.0	137.2
1985	124.5	134.8	106.6	143.0
1986	138.0	131.0	118.3	148.1

Source: World Bank, *World Tables* (Washington 1989–1990).

most puzzling differences is in the behavior of Thai real wages from 1983 to 1986. The ILO indicates a large increase after 1984 followed by a sharp decline, while the World Bank data suggest a gradual increase without annual fluctuations. The two sets are generally consistent in portraying wage growth in South Korea.

The reasons for these differences are not clear. The ILO statistics are derived from payroll surveys, while the World Bank statistics come from a United Nations Industrial Development Organization (UNIDO) data base. Both include earnings from overtime work, vacation pay, and taxes and social security payments, though the World Bank data include estimates of payments in kind while the ILO data do not. There are also some differences in the size of the enterprises covered. Unfortunately, neither set includes all the countries because of the absence of Malaysia and Taiwan.

Nevertheless, Tables 4.2 and 4.3 do enable us to get a rough picture of real wage changes in the five countries since 1970. South Korea and Taiwan, the first to develop, had fairly similar wage trends during the 1970s: 7.4 percent per annum for South Korea and 6.5 percent for Taiwan. The wage increases for Malaysia and

Thailand were much slower, 1.75 and 1.84 percent per annum respectively. After 1980, as the South Korean and Taiwanese economies became more mature and Malaysia and Thailand more industrialized, the rates grew closer: 4.6 percent and 6.8 percent annually for Malaysia and Thailand, and 5.6 and 6.0 percent for South Korea and Taiwan. From 1986 to 1989, South Korea out-paced Taiwan: 12.4 percent as against 7.7 percent.

These wage gains are impressive. A South Korean worker engaged in manufacturing would have seen his real wage quad-ruple over the two decades since 1970, while his colleague in Taiwan would have been paid more than three times as much at the end of the period than at the beginning. Both countries had begun to run out of cheap labor and there was pressure on wages from the supply side of the labor market. Malaysia and Thailand still have reserves in the form of unemployment or low wage farm labor, yet even their industrial labor force benefited from substan-tial real wage increases.

The Philippines were in a class by themselves. While the data for the 1970s are conflicting, the ILO statistics are probably correct in showing no wage increase from 1980 to 1986, a period in which the GDP actually fell. Money wage increases exceeded those in the other countries, but the Philippine worker had nothing to show for it.

Gains in real wages were not precisely equal to productivity increases, as Table 4.4 shows, but there was a rough correspon-dence between them.[1] Low productivity in the Philippines was accompanied by lagging real wages. In South Korea, Malaysia, and Taiwan, productivity gains tended to exceed those in wages, while there was not a great deal of difference between them in Thailand. This does suggest that market forces were at work in the determination of wages.

MALE-FEMALE WAGE DIFFERENTIALS

There is no *a priori* basis for predicting trends in male-female wage differentials during the course of economic development. The subject has been explored extensively in the United States

Table 4.4
Indexes of Ratios of Real Wages to Productivity[a] in Manufacturing
(1980 = 100)

	South Korea	Malaysia	Philippines	Taiwan	Thailand
1970	108.3	87.0	148.4	–	118.0
1975	80.1	83.1	97.8	88.5	115.1
1980	100	100	100	100	100
1981	87.1	94.0	113.6	95.3	101.6
1982	88.8	90.1	109.1	98.5	100.1
1983	88.3	87.4	104.4	92.1	98.9
1984	86.4	–	95.3	107.9	103.2
1985	89.0	–	101.6	99.5	104.0
1986	86.7	–	106.5	98.5	106.0
1987	–	–	–	97.4	–

Sources: Computed from World Bank, *World Tables* (Washington, 1989–1990); Republic
of China, *Taiwan Statistical Data Book* (Taipei, 1988).
[a]Defined as real output per employee in manufacturing

and other developed nations, and the jury is still out on the reasons for the differentials and for their persistence. Relative productivity, which is a product of many factors, undoubtedly plays a role, but the social status of women in the labor market is also important.

The data required even to begin to explore these questions are scarce, as a glance at Table 4.5 will demonstrate. Time series are available only for South Korea, Malaysia, and Taiwan. The Malaysian figures are clear: The relative wages of women rose during the course of development and by 1987 had reached the levels to which we are accustomed in the West. The data for Taiwan and South Korea tell somewhat different stories. There was remarkably little change from 1970 to 1989 in Taiwan. South Korean women did not do as well as their Taiwanese counterparts until 1989, when there was a sudden unusual leap in their status. This occurred in the context of the general nominal wage explosion of 1988–1989.

Table 4.5
Female Wages as a Percentage of Male Wages, 1970–1989

	South Korea[a]	Taiwan[a]	Malaysia[b] Malays	Chinese
1970	–	61.5	51	57
1975	47.4	–	–	–
1980	45.1	–	–	–
1981	45.2	65.9	–	–
1982	45.1	64.3	–	–
1983	46.2	64.3	–	–
1984	47.2	64.3	68	60
1985	46.9	63.2	–	–
1986	48.5	63.3	–	–
1987	50.3	63.8	65	63
1988	50.9	62.5	–	–
1989	60.3	61.2	–	–

Sources: International Labor Office, *Yearbook of Labor Statistics* (Geneva, 1990); Republic of China, *Monthly Bulletin of Earnings and Production Statistics* (Taipei, August 1990) Table 2; Dipak Mazumdar, *Malaysian Labor Markets Under Structural Adjustment* (Washington: World Bank, 1991), p. 68.
[a]Manufacturing
[b]All urban employees

The pre-1989 discrepancy between Taiwan and South Korea may have been a matter of composition; more women may have been employed in low-wage industries in South Korea than in Taiwan, which would tend to lower its average. For example, 8.4 percent of the South Korean manufacturing labor force was producing apparel in 1988 as against only 5.7 percent for Taiwan, although there was an offset in that apparel wages in South Korea were 83 percent of the average manufacturing wage against 76 percent for Taiwan. Textile wages in both countries were almost the same as the average for all manufacturing, so that this typically low-wage industry does not contribute to an explanation.[2] This line of inquiry cannot be pursued further because of insufficient data.

However, there are some data that do lend support to the hypothesis that the difference in the sex-earnings wage ratios between the

Table 4.6
Ratio of Female to Male Earnings, by Major Sector, 1988 (percent)

	South Korea	Taiwan
All industries	52.0	–
Mining	47.6	52.8
Manufacturing	52.1	62.3
Electric, gas	44.3	79.7
Construction	48.0	68.3
Commerce	56.5	66.7
Transport, communications	67.4	89.2
Finance, insurance, real estate	51.1	74.2
Services	57.5	66.3

Sources: Republic of Korea, *Yearbook of Labor Statistics* (Seoul, 1989), Table 33; Republic of China, *Yearbook of Labor Statistics* (Taipei, 1989), Table 53.

Table 4.7
Ratio of Female to Male Earnings, by Occupation, 1988 (percent)

	South Korea	Taiwan
All occupations	52.0	64.5
Professional and technical	63.1	67.8
Administrative and managerial	93.3	82.2
Clerical and related	54.6	62.9
Sales	53.3	65.5
Service	68.6	70.8
Agricultural	45.1	54.6
Production and related	55.6	57.4

Sources: Republic of Korea, *Yearbook of Labor Statistics* (Seoul, 1989), Table 33; Republic of China, *Yearbook of Labor Statistics* (Taipei, 1989), Table 58.

two countries are real phenomena rather than the product of statistical composition. These are contained in Tables 4.6 and 4.7. When the differentials are compared for all sectors of the economy rather than just manufacturing, the South Korean ratios are consistently lower. The same is true of occupational comparisons except in the case of administrative and managerial personnel, where the South Korean women have a relative advantage.

This leaves the basic question of causation unanswered. There may be sociological factors at work that determine the economic status of women, but that would require a study of its own. When data become available for the other countries, a more satisfactory conclusion to this interesting problem may be found.

WAGE STRUCTURE AND COMPOSITION

Overall wage averages conceal structural elements that are subject to variation over time. These include differentials by skill and by industry as well as various components of the wage packet.

In general, manufacturing wage differentials tend to narrow with economic growth. As industry becomes more capital intensive there is less need for unskilled labor, and workers who started in that category enter the ranks of the semiskilled. The supply of the latter category tends to decline as industry expands and unemployment falls. On the other end of the scale, the premium for skill tends to fall as education and training programs expand.

The same effects operate with respect to interindustry differentials. As labor becomes more expensive, the labor-intensive industries that are established at the onset of industrialization must either become more capital intensive or move offshore. As technological knowledge spreads, industries initially dependent on expensive foreign assistance are increasingly able to operate with indigenous employees. A good deal of the work that initially required highly skilled technicians can be done by semiskilled workers using more complex machinery.

Some data with which to test the skill hypothesis are shown in Table 4.8. The skill concepts are not uniform among the countries.

Table 4.8
Earnings Differentials by Skill (lower as a percentage of higher skills)

	South Korea [a]	Malaysia [b]	Philippines [c]	Taiwan [d]	Thailand [e]
1970		38.2			
1975	41.8 [f]			53.6	
1980	49.0		50.8	61.4 [h]	36.0
1985	54.0	49.5	56.2 [g]	63.8	
1987	58.1			65.5 [i]	
1988	61.7				
1990				72.1	

Sources: Republic of Korea, *Yearbook of Labor Statistics* (Seoul, various issues); Malaysia, *Survey of Manufacturing Industries* (Kuala Lumpur, various issues); Philippines, *Yearbook of Labor Statistics* (Manila, 1984); Republic of China, *Yearbook of Labor Statistics* (Taipei, various issues); Sadanja Nitungkorn, *Changing Labor Force of Thailand* (Bangkok, 1984), p. 112.
[a] Production workers/professional and technical employees
[b] Skilled workers/technical personnel in manufacturing
[c] Production workers/professional and technical employees, all industries
[d] Wage earners/salaried employees in manufacturing
[e] Production workers/professional and technical employees, all industries
[f] 1977
[g] 1983
[h] 1979
[i] 1986

For South Korea and the Philippines, the ratio of the earnings of production workers to those of professional and technical employees can serve as a rough index of skill differentials. For Malaysia, it is the ratio of skilled production workers to technical personnel in manufacturing. The best series is that for Taiwan, which compares the earnings of wage earners to salaried employees in manufacturing. Because of the difference in the groups compared, intercountry comparisons cannot be made.

In four countries (there is only a single observation for Thailand) the skill differential narrowed over time. In 15 years, it was down from 58 to 38 percent in South Korea and from 46 to 28 percent in Taiwan. The Malaysian decline was from 62 to 50 percent. Judging by the experience of South Korea and Taiwan, the premium for skill tends to decline fairly rapidly during the course of development.

The interindustry data are not as consistent. Wage dispersion in manufacturing, represented by coefficients of variation calculated from wages paid by individual industries, declined over time in South Korea and Malaysia, but rose in Taiwan (see Table 4.9). However, the latter counter-intuitive result is largely attributable to the fact that several industries that initially were very highly paid received large wage increases over the years covered. If the two highest-wage industries, petroleum products and chemical materials, are removed from the set of 20 industries, the variation coefficient falls from 0.18 in 1975 to 0.17 in 1988. It is a reasonable assumption that international differentials will tend to decline in the course of economic development.

Even in countries that are still in the early stages of development, a portion of earnings may be in the form of some fringe benefits that are essential if employees are to achieve a satisfactory level of performance. They may include transportation to and from the place of work if public transportation is not available; a nutritious midday meal; a medical and dental clinic; and even housing, particularly if the factory is not located in an urban center. As the economy grows, the composition of wages becomes more complex. The government may mandate certain payments, trade unions

Table 4.9
Coefficients of Variation of Manufacturing Wages among Industries

	South Korea	Malaysia	Taiwan
1975	0.28	0.63	0.21
1983		0.41	
1988	0.20		0.25

Sources: Republic of Korea, *Yearbook of Labor Statistics* (Seoul 1989), Table 32; Republic of China, *Yearbook of Labor Statistics* (Taipei, 1988), Table 52; World Bank data.

may gain them through collective bargaining, or the employer may initiate them as a means of stimulating productivity.

The situation at a fairly early stage of development is illustrated by the data for Thailand shown in Table 4.10. In the private sector, various payments in kind account for almost half of total earnings. In government service, cash remuneration is preponderant. The figures for Taiwan, which is much further along the development road, appear in Table 4.11. Payment in kind has disappeared and has been replaced by employer contributions to insurance, retirement, and welfare funds. The various goods and services provided by Thai employers are available to Taiwanese in the market. There is also remarkably little difference in the pay structure of salaried employees and wage earners, although wage earners put in more paid overtime and salaried personnel received higher bonuses.

Similarly detailed data are not available for South Korea, but it is known that South Korean employers follow a practice imported from Japan: the payment of large annual bonuses based upon enterprise profits. There have been instances in which bonuses came to a half a year's pay. The bonuses are not guaranteed, and are

Table 4.10
Composition of Earnings in Thailand, 1987 (percent of total)

	Government	Private
Total remuneration	100	100
Regular wages	62.1	31.3
Bonuses	2.5	12.5
Overtime	2.0	3.7
Other income	21.7	6.1
Food	0.3	19.1
Clothing	2.7	9.4
Housing	7.1	13.1
Transportation	1.6	4.8

Source: Thailand, *Statistical Yearbook* (Bangkok, 1989).

Table 4.11
Composition of Earnings in Taiwan, 1988 (percent of total)

	Average	Salaried workers	Wage earners
Total remuneration	100	100	100
Regular earnings	<u>81.2</u>	<u>81.2</u>	<u>81.2</u>
Basic earnings	73.4	73.8	73.2
Fixed allowances	5.0	5.3	4.9
Monthly bonuses	2.8	2.1	3.1
Irregular earnings	<u>12.4</u>	<u>12.5</u>	<u>12.3</u>
Overtime	3.7	2.4	4.4
Non-monthly bonus	7.4	8.9	6.6
Other allowances	1.3	1.2	1.3
Non-salary remuneration	<u>6.4</u>	<u>6.3</u>	<u>6.5</u>
Insurance paid by employer	3.0	2.7	3.1
Employer retirement fund contribution	2.0	2.2	2.0
Severance pay	0.3	0.3	0.4
Employer contribution to welfare fund	0.7	0.8	0.6
Other welfare outlays	0.4	0.3	0.4

Source: Republic of China, *Yearbook of Labor Statistics* (Taipei, 1988), Table 56.

not paid by all firms, but in 1981, for example, they constituted 14.4 percent of total earnings for all male employees and 19.4 percent for college graduates.[3] In general, South Korean wage structure is characterized by a relatively high proportion of earnings paid in the form of allowances rather than basic wages; 25 percent for white-collar and 39 percent for blue-collar workers. This enables employers to adjust wages more readily when economic circumstances change.[4] It may be noted that nonbasic wages are not insignificant in Malaysia—they amounted to 15 percent of

Table 4.12
Ratio of Minimum to Average Wages in Manufacturing, 1970–1988
(percent)

	South Korea	Philippines[a]	Taiwan	Thailand[d]
1970		64.1[e]	38.6	
1975		71.3	17.5	97[b]
1980		121.3	37.3	104
1985		88.9	48.8	92[c]
1988	35.6		48.2	

Sources: Korea and Taiwan: See Gee San, *An Evaluation and International Comparison of Labor Laws and Regulations Which Affect Labor Costs in Taiwan* (Chung-Hua Institution for Economic Research, 1989). Philippines: World Bank, *Philippines: A Framework for Economic Recovery* (Washington, 1987), p. 153; International Labor Office, *Yearbook of Labor Statistics* (Geneva, various issues). Thailand: International Labor Office, *Employment Issues and Policies for Thailand's Sixth Plan* (Geneva, 1985), pp. 52, 54.
[a]Ratio of highest minimum rate in Manila to average wages in nonagricultural activities
[b]1978
[c]1983
[d]Ratio of minimum wage to unskilled wage rate in manufacturing
[e]1972

earnings for male workers in 1984—but they are well below the South Korean level.

MINIMUM WAGES

Legislated minimum wages do not make much sense in developing countries. This is particularly true where unemployment or underemployment are severe, since enforcement becomes almost impossible. Yet most countries have adopted minimum wages, often because of pressure from the International Labor Organization. They are urged, however, to take employment considerations into account in fixing the minimum level, and this often makes them ineffective.

Available ratios between minimum wage rates and wages in manufacturing are shown in Table 4.12. Only for Taiwan in recent years do these ratios resemble those for developed countries. In the Philippines, minimum rates are set for 12 different categories of employers; the rates shown in the table are those for large firms in Manila, which would explain the high figures for 1980 and 1985. The South Korean Labor Ministry has had the authority to fix minimum wages for many years, but "apart from the brief experiment with minimum wage 'guidance' between 1975 and 1979, this power has not been exercised in even a formal way."[5] However, a minimum wage law was finally enacted in 1988 at a low relative level. The figures for Thailand, which compare the minimum with unskilled labor rates in manufacturing, reflect just what would be expected in newly developing countries: a close correspondence between minimum and actual wages, either because sufficient labor could be obtained at the minimum rate or because the government simply used market rates in fixing the minimum.

Minimum wages have recently become a controversial issue in the Philippines. Under union pressure the minimum was raised in 1989 by an average of 39 percent over the 1986 level. The unions claimed that this merely restored the real value of the 1984 level, while employers denounced the increase as inflationary.

However, this did not end the controversy because continuing inflation soon eroded the purchasing power of the new minimum wage level. In Manila, real wages declined by 10 percent from December, 1989, to June, 1990. The unions, the TUCP as well as the KMU, demanded a further increase in the minimum. The government refused, and argued that the 1989 legislation called for future increases to be set by regional councils, which in fact were not established until June, 1990. The employers maintained that the 1989 increase was the cause of the inflation. The Minister of Finance pointed out that manufacturing wages had risen by 220 percent since 1985.

Large employers were probably able to absorb the effect of the 1989 increase in the minimum wage, but smaller firms found it difficult to make the necessary adjustments. A check by the Labor Department indicated that 50 percent of these firms were not paying the minimum. It is claimed that as many as 20,000 workers lost their jobs as a result of imposing the 1989 level.[6]

HOURS OF WORK

Long hours of work are characteristic of developing countries. The normal work week is six days, and a nine-hour day is common. Overtime rates may be paid for more than 48 hours a week, but this is by no means universal. Table 4.13 shows working hours for the five Asian countries. They are not fully comparable, and some comment is required for each.

Long working hours have prevailed in South Korea for many years, and constituted a major input into its economic growth. According to a 1989 ILO report, Koreans worked the longest hours in the world in 1988. It is not unlikely that the recent labor protest in that country will lead to working hours that are more in keeping with its stage of development.

Table 4.13
Weekly Hours of Work in Manufacturing, 1970–1989

	South Korea	Malaysia	Philippines	Taiwan	Thailand
1970	52.3		44.2[d]		47.7
1975	50.5	44.0[b]	45.3	51.0[a]	
1980	53.1	47.0	46.2	51.0	
1985	53.8	45.6[c]	47.1	47.5	
1987	54.0		47.2		51
1988	52.6			46.5	51
1989	50.7			47.2	

Sources: International Labor Office, *Yearbook of Labor Statistics* (Geneva, 1988 and 1990); Republic of China, *Yearbook of Labor Statistics* (Taipei, 1988), Table 140; U.S. Department of Labor, *Foreign Labor Trends: Philippines* (Washington, 1989–90).
[a]1978
[b]Nonagricultural
[c]1984
[d]1971

Malaysians work considerably less. The standard work week is 44 hours, but many employers have moved down to 40 hours. However, the averages conceal wide divergences, since many workers put in longer hours. In 1986, 60 percent of all industrial employees put in 48 or more hours per week, at overtime rates over 44 hours.

The average work week in the Philippines during the late 1980s was 48 hours, and the surplus of available labor has made it unnecessary for employers to resort to overtime. A substantial proportion of the labor force works less than a full week; it has been estimated that in 1987, 30 percent of all employees worked less than 40 hours a week.

The growing shortage of labor in Taiwan that has contributed to rising incomes has also made employees less inclined to work long hours. The central government has instituted a 44-hour week for its employees, spread over 5-1/2 days, and some local governments went down to 5 days in 1990. Overtime rates are high and enforced, discouraging resort to this source of manpower.

Thai labor laws stipulate a standard working week of 48 hours for industrial employees, though overtime is permitted. In consequence, "a workweek of 48 to 56 hours is common in most occupations. Many Thai factories run on shifts; the customary length of a full-time shift is eight hours, regardless of whether it is the daytime or at night. On a shift where the work is intermittent, an employee may be required to work 10 hours."[7] Thailand is in the same class as South Korea when it comes to the number of hours its citizens are required to work.

What all this adds up to is that the five-day, 40-hour week that is standard among developed countries is still a long way off in the five Asian countries. Perhaps this is not surprising when it is recalled that Japanese industrial workers were still averaging a 47-hour week in 1988. Economic growth creates conflicting tendencies with respect to working hours. The rising demand for labor creates pressures for increasing working hours in order to maximize labor input. On the other hand, rising incomes induce employees to substitute leisure for work. In time, the latter tendency prevails, as the history of working conditions in developed countries demonstrates. How rapidly this occurs depends in part on the political and economic power that working people are able to exert. The 40-hour week is currently giving way in Europe; a major German strike in 1984 succeeded in making the first breach. How long it will take Asia to come down to 40 hours can only be guessed at; at least another decade of growth will probably be required.

NOTES

1. The data were computed by dividing an index of real earnings by an index of real output, per employee, both in manufacturing, as compiled by the World Bank.

2. The data are from Republic of China, *Yearbook of Labor Statistics* (Taipei, 1988), and Republic of Korea, *Yearbook of Labor Statistics* (Seoul, 1988).

3. David L. Lindauer, *Labor Market Behavior in the Republic of Korea* (Washington: World Bank, 1984), p. 52.

4. Se-il Park, "Labor Issues in Korea's Future," *World Development* vol. 16, no. 1 (1988): p. 115.

5. Ray Richardson and Byung Whan Kim, *Adjustments to Policy Changes: The Case of Korea, 1960–1985* (Washington: World Bank, October 1986), p. 11.

6. U.S. Department of Labor, *Foreign Labor Trends: Philippines* (Washington: GPO, 1988–1990), pp. 6–7.

7. Phiraphol Tritasavit, *Labor Policy and Practice in Thailand* (Ann Arbor, Michigan: University Microfilms, 1982), p. 57.

5

The State of Welfare

The goal of economic development is to increase the national supply of goods and services. There may be aberrant objectives for a time—for example, the building of military power in the interest of national security or foreign conquest—but eventually the success of a regime depends on how rapidly and how well it satisfies the aspirations of its citizens for a better life. People will work voluntarily and productively as long as they see some prospect of improving their living standards within a reasonable period of time. If this vision is denied them, the result is slackness and inefficiency, and eventually some form of chaos.

The acme of twentieth-century economic success is the modern welfare state. The hallmark of this type of regime is redistribution of income by the government to the less affluent members of society, financed by taxing the more affluent. Its purpose is to provide economic security from the cradle to the grave, and to eliminate poverty. The danger is that this policy may reduce work incentives with a consequent loss of dynamism, and lead to the sharing of a stagnant national product.

The Scandinavian countries, which have managed to achieve high per capita incomes despite limited natural resources, are generally included among those that are considered full-fledged welfare states. They are not the fastest growers among the developed nations, nor are they the wealthiest, but they have completely eliminated poverty, which must be accounted a remarkable achievement. What is most relevant to the subject of this book, they have provided their working people with a broad range of protective measures against economic disaster from unemployment, against deprivation caused by loss of income upon retirement, and against the adverse impact of accidents and illness.

Economic progress is usually charted by GNP growth or by growth of its various components, such as the output of industrial and agricultural products. The measurement of progress toward welfare is generally appended to the main economic series as "social indicators," a kind of footnote to the real thing. The World Bank, which has done a great deal to highlight the welfare aspects of development, issued in 1989 a volume entitled *Social Indicators of Development*, a publication that it rightly called "a quantum leap over what has been previously published."[1] There is still a way to go before comprehensive data are available for all the developing countries, but the problems involved in assessing what I have termed the state of welfare in the five Asian countries are considerably reduced by the World Bank's initiative.

It might also be pointed out that the 1990 edition of the World Bank's annual *World Development Report* is titled "Poverty," and is the most comprehensive catalog of this unfortunate circumstance that has ever been compiled. The report points out that "mortality among children under 5 in South Asia exceeds 170 deaths per thousand; in Sweden it is fewer than 10," and argues that "progress in raising average incomes, however welcome, must not distract attention from [the] massive and continuing burden of poverty."[2]

INCOME DISTRIBUTION

The growth of the national product discussed in Chapter 1 tells only part of the welfare story. The distribution of income is a crucial factor in determining whether growth has contributed to the general welfare. Redistribution of income and wealth alone may improve living standards, but the improvement is likely to be moderate at best. Redistribution *with* growth is a more promising formula.

The trend of income distribution over time can tell a great deal. If the share of the lower-income groups is increasing, there is strong evidence of the beneficial effects of economic growth. If it is declining, the growth dividend is being siphoned off by the wealthier, and poverty may actually be increasing.

Income distributions for four of the five Asian countries, from 1970 to various years in the 1980s, are contained in Table 5.1. (Recent data for Thailand are not available.) They take the form of proportions of national income received by the various income classes. The Gini coefficients, which measure inequality (the higher the coefficient, the greater the inequality) are also shown, together with the ratio of the income received by the top 20 percent income class to the bottom 20 percent class. It should be added that these are estimates to be taken with caution.

Mainly through the work of Simon Kuznets, it has been hypothesized that in the early stages of economic development, income distribution tends to become more unequal, while at some later stage, this tendency is reversed. For the period 1970 to 1982, South Korean income distribution worsened. It is possible that the turning point may have been reached after 1982, though there are no data to substantiate this. In Taiwan, however, the tremendous growth that took place from 1970 to 1988 was accomplished with almost no change in income distribution, an event that has been acclaimed in several studies.[3] Malaysia, which is at an earlier stage of development than South Korea and Taiwan, suffered a deterioration of income equality over the two decades,

Table 5.1

Income Distribution by Income Class (percent received by each income class)

	South Korea		Malaysia		Philippines		Taiwan	
	1970	1982	1970	1987	1971	1988	1970	1988
Top 20%	41.6	43.0	40	51.2	54.0	51.7	38.7	38.2
Next 20%	38.8[a]	38.2[a]	49[a]	21.2	21.0	20.7	22.5	22.9
Middle 20%				13.9	13.3	13.3	17.1	17.6
Next 20%	19.6[b]	18.8[b]	7	9.3	8.1	9.1	13.3	13.4
Low 20%			4	4.6	3.6	5.2	8.4	7.9
Gini coeff- icients	.332	.357	–	.386	.401	.386	.321	.321

Sources: South Korea: Tony Mitchell, *From a Developing to a Newly Industrialized Country: the Republic of Korea* (Geneva, ILO, 1988); Jang-ho Kim, *Wages, Employment and Income Distribution in South Korea* (New Delhi: ARTEP, 1986), p. 75. Malaysia: World Bank, *Social Indicators of Development* (Washington, 1990), p. 193; World Bank, *World Development Report* (Washington, 1990), p. 237. Philippines: *Philippine Statistical Yearbook* (Manila 1989), Table 2–8. Taiwan: Shirley W. Y. Kuo, *Conference on Economic Development: Experience of Taiwan* (Taipei: Institute of Economics, 1988), p. 85; Republic of China, *Statistical Yearbook* (Taipei, 1989), Table 68.

[a]Second and third highest 20%
[b]Lowest 40%

with no sign of a turn. The Philippines have made some progress toward greater equality, although its Gini coefficient indicates a very unequal initial distribution.

The data suggest that economic growth is likely eventually to lead to greater income equality, though the findings are not unambiguous. Growth certainly improves the absolute level of welfare, but it may not be sufficient in itself to bring about the equalization of incomes.

OCCUPATIONAL SAFETY AND HEALTH

In the early stages of industrialization, little attention is paid
to the health and safety of working people in the struggle of
employers to survive and of workers to escape from grinding
poverty. As firms become more profitable and the supply of labor
more abundant, there is greater concern for improvement in the
conditions under which work is performed. Industrial accidents
become less frequent as safety measures are introduced and
dangerous materials are banned. Improvement tends to be slow,
however; even in the most advanced countries they are often
matters of contention.

The available statistics for the Asian countries on the rate of
work injuries in manufacturing are shown in Table 5.2. It is
important to note that these rates are not comparable among
countries, since they differ in terms of reporting requirements and
the employment base. Although the period covered by the data is

Table 5.2
**Injuries in Manufacturing Establishments (ratio of total injuries to total
employment)**

	South Korea	Malaysia	Taiwan	Thailand
1975	.050		.014[a]	
1980	.034	.045	.013	.011
1985	.033	.036	.013	.014
1987	.028	.034	.008	.013
1988	.027			

Sources: International Labor Office, *Yearbook of Labor Statistics* (Geneva: various
issues); Korea, *Yearbook of Labor Statistics* (Seoul, 1989); Malaysia, *Labor Indicators* (Kuala Lumpur, 1985–1986); Republic of China, *Yearbook of Labor Statistics* (Taipei, 1988).
[a]1978

Table 5.3
Health Indicators

	25–30 years ago	15–20 years ago	Most recent estimate
South Korea			
Population per physician	2684	2200	1166
Population per nurse	2972	1190	587
Population per hospital bed	–	1900	600
Malaysia			
Population per physician	6202	4283	1935
Population per nurse	1316	1269	1013
Population per hospital bed	–	299	480
Philippines			
Population per physician	–	9100	6700
Population per nurse	1130	2687	2741
Population per hospital bed	–	600	600
Taiwan			
Population per physician	1901	1492	1016
Population per nurse	–	–	–
Population per hospital bed	2851	526	228
Thailand			
Population per physician	7159	8394	6294
Population per nurse	4971	1171	713
Population per hospital bed	–	899	–

Sources: World Bank, *Social Indicators of Development* (Washington, 1989); *Taiwan Statistical Data Book* (Taipei, 1988), Table 15.3.

not long, there is a clear downward trend in accident rates in South Korea, Malaysia, and Taiwan, though not in Thailand. The rapid decline in the incidence of accidents in South Korea is of particular interest.

Health indicators for employees, particularly those in manufacturing, are not generally available for the five Asian countries. There are some for the population as a whole, though they are not completely satisfactory for our purposes because they include the farm as well as the urban population. They are worth looking at, however, because they do say something about the relationship between economic growth and health.

It appears from the data in Table 5.3 that over a period of two to three decades, South Korea and Taiwan made great strides toward better health care for their citizens as measured by the availability of physicians and hospital facilities. They are far more advanced in this respect than any of their Asian neighbors except Japan. Malaysia moved from a relatively low to a respectable level during the past few years. There was some progress in Thailand as well, though the general level remains backward. The number of Philippine physicians increased in recent years; many of those who were trained migrated to the United States. The other indicators, however, show no progress. On the whole, scarce as they are, the data support the conclusion that economic growth does help increase the availability of health facilities.

SOCIAL SECURITY

Along with higher wages and protection against occupational hazards, economic development normally provides wage earners with some insurance against losses of income due to unemployment and retirement. These are usually minimal at the outset of development and tend to become more substantial as the economy prospers. Eventually they amount to a sizable increment to wages, reaching as much as a quarter of total income in developed countries.

Taiwan has gone further in this respect than the other Asian countries. The basic legislation is the Labor Standards Law of 1984, with the following major provisions:

1. Severance pay. This is payable to a discharged employee at the rate of one month's salary for every year of service. This payment may appear to be generous in an international context, but in fact it is a substitute for unemployment compensation. The cost is borne by the employer.

2. Pensions. An employee may qualify for a pension from two sources: directly from the employer or from the government pursuant to the Labor Insurance Act. In the event of voluntary retirement, a worker who has reached the age of 55 years and has worked continuously with an enterprise for at least 15 years is entitled to a lump-sum pension equal to two months of average wages for the first 15 years worked plus one month for each additional year, up to a maximum of 45 months of wages. If the employer terminates the employment before the 15-year requirement is met, the employee receives severance pay rather than the pension. In the case of a voluntary quit before the 15-year service period, nothing is payable.

The state pension, which is financed by employer and employee contributions to a state fund, is payable to an employee who reaches the retirement age at the rate of one month's average pay for each year of insured work, up to a maximum of 45 months. This means that a retired worker could be eligible for 90 months pay under the combined systems.

This seemingly generous pension system, which at first blush appears to place a heavy burden on Taiwan's employers, is subject to several qualifications. Labor turnover rates are high, so that many workers do not build up the necessary service years. Also, many firms in Taiwan are small and do not remain in existence for 15 years. This means that workers are more likely to receive several severance payments during their working careers than pensions. However, employers are required to establish a pension fund to which they must contribute specified percentages of their wage bills regardless of the retirement status of their employees, so that eligible employees will receive some pensions even if their firms go out of business.[4] It has been estimated that the severance and pension provisions add between 10 and 23 percent to the average firm's monthly wage cost, depending on the characteristics of its labor force.[5]

Several additional programs might be mentioned. A female worker is entitled to an 8-week maternity leave before and after childbirth. If she has been employed for 6 months or longer, she receives her regular wage; if less than 6 months, half the wage. There is also a mandatory year-end bonus to workers who have been with a company for the entire year, paid out of profits after provision for taxes and dividends. The law does not fix the precise amount, but many private employers follow the government practice of giving a month's extra pay to its employees. So-called labor insurance covers hospitalization, work-related injuries and illness, and disability. By 1989, 83 percent of the labor force was covered by maternity leave and labor insurance provisions.

South Korean employees are entitled to one month's severance pay for each year worked with the same employer, whether termination is due to layoff, voluntary quit, or retirement. South Korea did not have a national pension system until 1988, and the law enacted that year will not be extended to the entire labor force until 1995. A national medical insurance system covers about 45 percent of outpatient costs and 80 percent of hospital costs, but it has been badly underfunded. There is also a 60-day maternity leave. South Korea lags well behind Taiwan in the area of social security. Not until the Roh government came into office and labor unrest grew was relevant legislation enacted. But the World Bank notes that "the Korean government will be focusing increasingly on social development especially as democratization progresses. This emphasis on social expenditure increase to improve the standard of living of low-income households is clearly indicated in the Sixth Five Year Plan."[6]

There is no unemployment compensation in Malaysia, but there is a requirement of severance pay of from 10 to 20 days per year of service. However, there are surprisingly liberal social security benefits, as shown in Table 5.4. The basis is an Employee Provident Fund that goes back to 1951, which receives a contribution from the employee equal to 9 percent of wages, and from the employer, 11 percent. Each individual employee has a separate account, which is also credited with accrued interest. The amount accumulated may be withdrawn by the employee at age 55, or in the event of disability or emigration from the country. Under a 1986 amendment, workers may withdraw up to 40 percent of the price of a low-

Table 5.4
Social Security in Malaysia, 1980, 1988

	Persons Receiving Social Security Benefits	
	1980	1988
Temporary disability	9613	51718
Permanent disability	587	3006
Dependants' benefits	3502	6589
Funeral benefits	124	1413
Other	94	12094
Total	13920	74820

Activities of the Social Security Organization		
Number of employees registered	1706170	3731525
Industrial accidents reported	51340	88127
Accidents receiving medical benefits	48503	83801

Source: Malaysia, *Yearbook of Labor Statistics* (Bangkok, 1988), Tables 15.4 and 15.5.

cost house or 20 percent of a more expensive one. Fund membership at the end of 1988 was over 5 million, a large proportion of the eligible labor force.

There is a separate pension system for civil servants, financed entirely by the government. In 1987, the government decided to move all new employees into the general system in order to reduce the cost, but there was so much protest that this decision was rescinded.

The Social Security Organization also provides payment for full or partial disability, equal to 50 to 65 percent of previous earnings, depending on previous length of service. Another insurance scheme pays medical and disability benefits arising from work-related injury or disease. These are very generous: 80 percent of the previous wage for temporary disability and 90 percent for permanent disability.[7]

At the beginning of 1990, Thailand had no national social security system. The only operative program was a workmen's compensation fund covering job-connected injuries and deaths. The government proposed a modest social security law in 1988 to provide insurance against sickness, disability, and nonemployment related injuries, initially covering only 300,000 workers. This legislation was approved by the lower house of parliament in 1989 and was due to be approved by the Senate in 1990.

However, employees dismissed without cause have been entitled to severance pay since 1974, the amount ranging from one to six month's wages depending on previous employment tenure. In addition, some firms provide such welfare benefits as medical care, life and retirement insurance, and financing assistance for home construction. However, most Thai employees still lack basic social protections.

The Philippines have long had one of the best codes of social legislation to be found in any developing country (see Table 5.5). A national pension system dates back to 1954, covering all employees and the self-employed earning more than a specified minimum income. It is contributory, with employees paying from 1.3 to 3.3 percent of earnings and employers paying from 5.1 to 6.8 percent of payroll. The pension is payable at age 60 if there have been 120 months of contributions.

The social security system also provides benefits for illness and temporary disability equal to 90 percent of the previous year's earnings. The sickness benefit can be drawn upon after a three-day waiting period up to a maximum of 120 days in a calendar year, while temporary disability due to an accident is compensable immediately and can run for 240 days. Permanent disability benefits are calculated in the same manner as pensions, and can be taken in a lump sum equal to 35 months of the pension amount. Maternity benefits run for 45 days at 100 percent of previous wages. There are also survivor benefits for spouses and minor children.

Table 5.5
Social Security in the Philippines, 1970, 1980, 1988

| | Benefits paid (thousand pesos) | | |
	1970	1980	1988
Death	10650	111656	1076238
Disability	2579	30485	274581
Sickness	19118	63322	315993
Retirement	16549	183502	1194789
Maternity	-	37851	189728
Medicare	-	203831	474474

Workers and employers covered by Social Security and Medicare
(thousands)

	Workers	Employers
1970	2574	91
1980	8058	231
1988	10792	296

Source: Philippine Statistical Yearbook (Manila 1989), Table 12.5.

There is no unemployment compensation system, but termination of employment due to technological change or several other reasons for redundancy is compensable at the rate of one month's pay for each year of service. Medical expenses are provided subject to limitations set by the Employees' Compensation Commission.

This is an advanced protective code for a country at the Philippine level of development, but there are some problems with it. One involves administration; safety and health legislation, for example, has been on the books for some years, but little attention was paid to it during the Marcos regime. From 1978 to 1987, no labor standard inspections were carried out, and when the Aquino government began looking at factories it found that 40 percent of those inspected were in gross violation of the law. In 1989, however, twice as many inspections were carried out as in 1988, and the number of violations increased tenfold. Whatever else it is not doing, the Aquino regime is moving positively on the worker protection front.[8]

A more fundamental problem stems from the country's high rates of unemployment and underemployment. Since social security is tied to employment, a substantial proportion of the population has no access to it. Only about half the labor force was covered in 1988. There is widespread poverty; it was estimated that in 1985, 52 percent of all families were below the government-established poverty standard, and despite some improvement in economic conditions, almost half the families were still below the poverty limit in 1988. The causes of poverty were the same as those that frustrated economic development: poor management of the economy and low agricultural productivity combined with rapid population growth.

It is clear that economic development is not automatically accompanied by greater social security. Taiwan has an extensive system, but South Korea, at about the same level of development, does not. Malaysia provides generous social protection but Thailand does not. The Philippines are a special case—a fair degree of protection for those who are employed amidst a sea of unemployment and poverty.

None of the five countries has as yet instituted unemployment compensation, but some form of severance pay serves as a substitute. Workmens' compensation laws appear to be universal. One interesting finding is the fairly widespread existence of maternity benefits under circumstances where population limitation is national policy.

A few additional social indicators appear in Table 5.6. Newspaper circulation increased with the spread of education except for South Korea, which had a widespread readership at the onset of development. Telephones and passenger cars were also much more available after several decades of growth. The Philippines lagged behind in both respects.

Table 5.6
Social Indicators of Development

	25-30 years ago	15-20 years ago	Most recent estimate
Newspaper circulation (per thousand population)			
South Korea	63.2	170.3	145.8
Malaysia	566	84.7	173.3
Philippines	17.8	15.9	36.9
Thailand	13.0	21.6	51.6
Population per telephone (persons)			
South Korea	-	25	4
Malaysia	-	42	11
Philippines	-	96	66
Taiwan	76	14	3
Thailand	-	133	52
Population per passenger car (persons)			
South Korea	1750	332	74
Malaysia	60	26	11
Philippines	232	112	155
Taiwan	842	111	13
Thailand	455	155	74

Sources: World Bank, *Social Indicators of Development* (Washington 1989); Republic of China, *Statistical Yearbook* (Taipei 1989), Tables 218, 224.

To summarize, the five Asian countries are a long way from being modern welfare states. Economic growth certainly brings about a substantial improvement in the living and working conditions of the labor force, but progress is not a simple function of the rate of growth. Social security standards appear to be influenced by a nation's preindustrial customs and traditions, to say nothing of its political system.

It is not possible to pinpoint the precise level of development at which social programs are efficient. It would appear that in at least four of our five Asian countries, some social measures were not in conflict with the conditions that made growth possible. Developing countries can be encouraged to improve their social benefit structures if the availability of resources and administrative capacity make it possible to translate legislation into reality.

NOTES

1. World Bank, *Social Indicators of Development* (Washington, 1989), p. v.

2. World Bank, *World Development Report* (Washington, 1990), p. 1.

3. Shirley Y. W. Kuo, "The Achievement of Growth With Equity," *Conference on Economic Development Experience of Taiwan* (Taipei: Institute of Economics, 1988), p. 71; John C. H. Fei, Gustav Ranis, and Shirley W. Y. Kuo, *Growth With Equity: The Taiwan Case* (World Bank, 1979).

4. See Gee San, *A Critical Review of the Labor Standards Law in Taiwan, R.O.C.* (Taipei: Chung-Hua Institution for Economic Research, December, 1988); and See Gee San, *An Evaluation and International Comparison of Labor Laws and Regulations Which Affect Labor Costs in Taiwan* (Taipei: Chung-Hua Institution for Economic Research, February, 1989).

5. See Gee San, *An Evaluation*, p. 36.

6. World Bank, *Trends in Developing Economies* (Washington, 1990), p. 300.

7. U.S. Department of Labor, *Foreign Labor Trends: Malaysia*, (Washington: GPO, 1988–1989), pp. 10–11.

8. U.S. Department of Labor, *Foreign Labor Trends: Philippines*, (Washington: GPO, 1988–1989), p. 18, and 1989–1990, p. 13.

6

Conclusions

This study has explored some of the relationships between economic growth and labor market changes in the course of growth. The results lead to the conclusion that in the main, the five Asian nations included in the study—South Korea, Malaysia, the Philippines, Taiwan, and Thailand—have followed the trails blazed earlier by the presently industrialized nations of the world. There are some differences that may be due to political and cultural factors, but basic economic forces appear to be determining except where they are frustrated by counter-productive government intervention.

South Korea and Taiwan have been the world-champion growers during the last quarter of a century, their speed of development matched only by that of Japan. Malaysia and Thailand started later and advanced less rapidly, though during the 1980s they also emerged as world-class players. The Philippines are the laggards, held back by factors described above.

The first thing to be observed is that manpower has not been a constraint on development. All five countries were "overpopulated" to begin with, with large cohorts of unskilled labor inured to hard work, mainly in low-productivity agriculture. High rates of population growth combined with high rates of labor-force participation served to keep the manpower pool full, though this changed with the decline of population growth attendant upon industrialization and urbanization. All the countries were fortunate in having good educational systems fairly early on, particularly at the elementary level. The continuing supply of workers who could acquire skills quickly fueled the growth process.

The contribution of women was another major factor. As men migrated to the cities and secured industrial jobs, the women remained behind to maintain farm production. Those who already lived in the cities, or near enough to commute daily (Taiwan provides a good example of this pattern), left their households in increasing numbers to enter paid employment, while at the same time continuing to carry the burdens of their domestic obligations. By the end of the 1980s, they constituted from 40 to 45 percent of the manufacturing labor force in these countries, and predominated in commercial activities.

Lack of skills is sometimes cited as an obstacle to development, but this does not appear to have been the case in our five Asian countries. Investment in secondary and higher education was sufficient to provide an adequate flow of the manpower required by changing technology. There was some foreign assistance in the setting up of training facilities, but domestic institutions provided the necessary skill training, both classroom and on the job.

Philippine manpower experience may serve as a warning to government administrators in the less-developed countries. Although the Philippines averaged annual GDP growth of almost 6 percent from 1965 to 1980, the percentage of the labor force employed in manufacturing failed to rise, in sharp distinction to what happened in the other countries. This was due to a governmentally inspired bias in favor of capital-intensive industries at a time when the Philippines should have been taking advantage of their cheap labor to embrace labor intensity. Indeed, the failure of the manufacturing employment sector to increase its relative share of total employment during the early stages of development might well be taken as a signal of faulty investment policies.

The bane of less-developed countries is the lack of sufficient productive jobs. Anyone who has worked or traveled in these countries has seen the familiar signs: the presence of a great many people engaged in marginal occupations. Among them are the selling of lottery tickets and cheap goods; transportation of goods and people by human power alone; and other activities that are close to begging. The point is that everyone must do something if he or she is to survive, for there are usually no income support systems available. Under such conditions, unemployment is not a useful concept, and the statistics published by many developing countries are meaningless. What does prevail is underemployment—very low-productivity jobs—and this is impossible to measure. The unemployment statistics for early years that appear in Table 2.13 must be taken with more than the customary grain of salt.

One of the most impressive achievements of economic growth is to reduce and eventually eliminate underemployment and to make the unemployment figures a realistic reflection of slack in the labor market. People in marginal occupations are drawn into productive employment, labor supply and demand become more balanced. Whether the 1989 unemployment rates of 2.6 percent for South Korea and 1.6 percent for Taiwan would pass muster in the U.S. Bureau of Labor Statistics is debatable, but the upward adjustment to make them conform to Western standards would be far less than would have been necessary two decades ago. Indeed, Taiwan has been importing unskilled labor, much of it illegal. The precise correlation between economic growth and declining unemployment cannot be determined from the available data, but there can be no doubt that the best and perhaps only cure for the endemic underemployment in the less-developed countries is growth; the faster the better, particularly when the capital-labor ratios of new industries are determined by relative market prices of the two factors of production.

General conclusions about structural institutions of the labor market do not emerge as clearly. Any system of industrial relations has many facets: the manner in which employees are represented in their dealings with management, the methods and scope of collective bargaining, the degree of government intervention. One of the problems is that trade unions are potentially important political as well as economic organizations, and autocratic governments tend to be wary of the challenges to their authority that may arise if unions are permitted to gain strength.

One of the questions raised at the outset of this study was whether trade unions and collective bargaining impede economic growth. Unfortunately, the experience of the five Asian countries does not provide an answer for the simple reason that the unions were either weak or nonexistent for most of the years under review. Conditions of labor were determined unilaterally by employers with or without the assistance of government. However, some interesting changes took place in the late 1980s, and their effects, while not yet entirely clear, are worth noting.

To recapitulate the current status of trade unions very briefly, the South Korean unions first began to gain independence and strength in 1987. Prior to this they were powerless and under the thumb of the government. The same was true in Taiwan, beginning a year later. The early trade unions in the Philippines were stifled by Marcos, and only when he was ousted in 1986 did they begin to revive, although they are split along ideological lines. The military governments that have ruled Thailand for most of the postwar years did not look upon unions with favor. The elected government that came into office in 1988 offered them some hope, but the military who took over in 1991 have already indicated that they may dissolve the unions in the nationalized industries, where they are best organized. Only in Malaysia have trade unions led a legal existence for the past two decades, although they have been handicapped by Malay-Chinese conflict and by the relatively small size of enterprises, making it difficult to organize.

A smoothly functioning system of industrial relations can make a significant contribution to productivity. Many conditions of labor apart from wages can lead to employee discontent. Without some mechanism for handling grievances, an employer may face slowdowns and interruptions in the work process. Strikes are by no means the only way in which employee discontent can be manifested.

It is of course possible to have satisfactory industrial relations wihout independent trade unions. Company unions dominated by the employer may nevertheless provide an adequate outlet for the expression of grievances. Employees may be consulted either in groups or individually to provide some input into managerial decisions. The government may establish mediation or arbitration tribunals to which employees may protest employer actions.

Of our five Asian countries, only Malaysia has had a relatively stable system of industrial relations throughout the last two decades, perhaps as a residue of the institutions established when Malaysia was a British colony. Labor strife has been low, enterprise-level collective bargaining has operated within the bounds prescribed by legislation. A contributing factor was the paternal attitude of the Malay-dominated governments toward the predominantly Malay industrial and rubber plantation labor force, manifested in the so called *Bhumiputra* program, which was designed to increase the share of the Malays in the economic pie.

The other countries managed with little in the way of formal industrial relations. A free labor market with little to hinder it prevailed in South Korea and Taiwan, although some employers did consult informally with their employees, particularly in Taiwan. The impact of the government-regulated system established in Thailand in 1975 has been minimal. The Philippines have had an elaborate labor code modeled on that of the United States, but it has functioned only sporadically, depending on the nature of the government in power.

Why should a developing country concern itself with trade unions, collective bargaining, and labor relations legislation? South Korea and Taiwan achieved almost unbelievable rates of economic growth by letting entrepreneurs manage their working forces as they saw fit. They obviously paid wages that were sufficient to acquire and retain the workers they needed. Would not unions have raised wages above true market levels, reduced profits, and eventually impaired investment funds? Should not their experience provide a labor model for less-developed nations?

One answer to this question is that entrepreneurs devoted to rapid expansion of their firms and backed by authoritarian governments can indeed follow the Asian model. They can count upon a quiescent workforce during the early stages of development when there is a surplus of labor. People who manage to find steady jobs at this juncture have hit the jackpot, and are not likely to do anything that might endanger their continued employment. There are too many unemployed waiting in the wings to replace them.

But the situation changes when a balanced labor market is attained, making it more difficult for an employer to replace dissident employees, when wages have reached a level enabling workers to sustain themselves on their savings for at least short periods of time and to support unions by dues payments. Demands for greater political democracy begin to emerge as people become more affluent. Resentment over working conditions that were stifled in the past can now be expressed openly. Strikes and other forms of job action, sometimes violent, multiply.

South Korea provides the best example of this scenario. The data in Table 3.1 show the enormous increase in strikes that began in 1987 after years of almost complete labor peace. This was costly to the economy. A recent publication of the World Bank noted that the disappointingly low growth of the national product in 1989 was due to two major factors: appreciation of the South Korean currency relative to the U.S. dollar and "large wage increases, workplace stoppages, and labor productivity decline owing to labor strife during the last two years."[1]

Similar political and economic developments in Taiwan have also led to an upsurge of labor activity there, though not as explosive as in South Korea. The Taiwanese unions are not yet strong enough to mount widespread strikes, employers are taking a very tough line, and the government still maintains strong controls over union activity. It is difficult to predict what will happen when political parties in opposition to the ruling Kuomintang gain strength, but an explosion on the labor front cannot be ruled out.

The situation in Malaysia provides a sharp contrast with what is happening in South Korea and Taiwan. Although the Malaysian trade unions have organized about one-quarter of the workers in manufacturing as well as most plantation workers, government regulation has hobbled them. Nevertheless, collective bargaining is well established and collective agreements, often of long duration, are in effect. This tends to reduce the pressure for direct action.

The conclusion is that while there are undoubted benefits from untrammeled labor markets in the early stages of economic development, failure to install an orderly system of industrial relations may entail serious costs later on. There is a price to be paid for autocratic rule, in employment relations as elsewhere.

Turning to wages, it should come as no surprise to learn that real wages rose rapidly in South Korea and Taiwan, more slowly but nonetheless consistently in Malaysia and Thailand, and very little in the Philippines. Except for the Philippines, all the countries managed to keep inflation in check by confining money wage increases roughly to increases in labor productivity. The wage gains achieved by manufacturing employees in South Korea and Taiwan were particularly impressive; over the two decades beginning in 1970 they rose by a factor of four in South Korea and by not much less in Taiwan. The most rapid increases took place during the 1980s when the supply of labor began to dry up.

The evolution of wage structure conformed to that of the industrial nations. By 1970, Taiwan was not far from the Biblical two-thirds ratio of female to male wages. South Korea started much lower at 47 percent in 1975 but reached 60 percent by 1989. Western scholars have devoted a great deal of time and effort in attempts to determine the persistently lower female wage levels that prevail almost everywhere, but there are no widely accepted conclusions. The feminists cite discrimination and advocate affirmative action, while others tend to rely on the theory of marginal productivity.

Most wage differentials tend to narrow with economic growth, and so they have in Asia. With the spread of education and a diminishing supply of unskilled labor, low-wage industries find it necessary to raise compensation in order to attract employees. An increased supply of skilled workers enables more technologically advanced industries to get along with relatively lower increases. The Asian experience in this respect is not completely unambiguous. While interindustrial wage differentials clearly narrowed over time in South Korea and Malaysia, they widened somewhat in Taiwan. However, the latter finding appears to have been due to anomolous circumstances in two high-wage industries that are not large employers. Wage differentials for skill behaved as expected in the four countries for which data are available: they narrowed.

It is a feature of wage structure in less-developed countries that a substantial portion of wages are paid in the form of noncash benefits and irregular cash distributions. The reason is that the markets for many essential goods and services are thin so that some items can be supplied more readily by the employer. This is best illustrated by the data for Thailand in Table 4.10, from which it appears that as late as 1987, less than one-third of private sector earnings were paid in the form of regular cash wages, with food, clothing, and housing contributing an additional 40 percent. Taiwan was at the other end of the spectrum; more than 80 percent of earnings came in the form of regular payments. Payments in kind had disappeared, though employers had begun to make contributions to various welfare schemes.

Minimum wages do not have much relevance in less-developed countries. Only when a fairly high income level is reached do they play any role in wage determination. The minimum wage legislation enacted by all five Asian countries may have served the twin purpose of convincing workers that the government was looking out for their welfare and winning kudos from the international community.

Hours of work have been long and have not been reduced as rapidly as might have been expected. South Korea had particularly long hours: a 52-hour week in 1970 and only a small reduction by

1989. Workers did better in Taiwan, with 47 hours in 1989, down from 51 hours in 1975. It is rather remarkable that Malaysia was down to 45.6 hours in 1984. There may be some Asian influence in this pattern of working hours; many Japanese still do not enjoy a five-day work week.

Finally, welfare. Well-being is of course closely related to earnings, but it is not the only factor that should be taken into account. Income distribution is another. Even if the national income rises, increasing inequality of income distribution may deprive the poorer segment of the population of the fruits of development. The absolute income of that group may rise, but there still may be strong resentment against the rich getting relatively richer.

The Kuznets hypothesis, that income distribution worsens in the early stages of development and turns toward equality later on, is borne out by the experience of South Korea and Malaysia. But Taiwan is an exception. It is a famous case of "growth with equity" for reasons that are not entirely clear. An equalizing trend appears to have occurred in the Philippines without growth, but the data are suspect.

Factory safety and health facilities should improve with economic growth, and they do in our sample of Asian countries. Among other things, they contribute to productivity. However, social benefits and services such as pensions, unemployment compensation, and disability insurance tend to be introduced very slowly, although severance pay in lieu of unemployment benefits are common fairly early on. Taiwan has the best social security system of the group, as befits its advanced status, but South Korea, which is as far along economically, lags far behind. Malaysia has a surprisingly good system, Thailand almost none. The Philippines have a generous code of social legislation, but its administration leaves a great deal to be desired.

It can be argued that to burden a developing country too early with expensive welfare benefits may frustrate growth. But this ignores the plight of its working people, who face the possibility of unemployment and the certainty of retirement with nothing to fall back on. There may be a trade-off between the rate of economic growth and the welfare of the labor force, at least in the short run. At any rate, the social security systems adopted by Taiwan and Malaysia do not appear to have retarded their development.

South Korea and Taiwan are now considered to be among the industrialized nations of the world, while Malaysia and Thailand are moving rapidly in that direction. Their economies are dynamic, and their labor conditions can be expected to improve, exceeding those in some Eastern and Southern European countries in the not distant future, for example. To quote a recent World Bank publication dealing with poverty, the best strategy for improving the quality of life for the poor "is the pursuit of a pattern of growth that ensures productive use of the poor's most abundant asset—labor," as well as "widespread provision to the poor of basic social services, especially primary education, primary health care, and family planning."[2] This is not a bad description of the strategy followed by four of our five Asian countries. The penalty for failure to adopt this prescription is exemplified by the unfortunate state of affairs that prevails in the Philippines.

NOTES

1. World Bank, *Trends in Developing Economies* (Washington, 1990), p. 299.

2. World Bank, *World Development Report* (Washington, 1990), p. iii.

Bibliography

China (Republic of). *Monthly Bulletin of Earnings and Production Statistics*. Taipei, various issues.
——— . *Taiwan Statistical Data Book*. Taipei, various issues.
——— . *Statistical Yearbook*. Taipei, various issues.
——— . *Yearbook of Labor Statistics*. Taipei, various issues.
——— . *Yearbook of Manpower Statistics*. Taipei, various issues.
Denoon, David B. H. *Constraints on Strategy*. McLean, VA: Pergamon Brassey, 1986.
Dornbusch, Rudiger, and Yung Chai Park. "Korean Growth Policy." *Brookings Papers on Economic Activity*, vol. 2. Washington: Brookings Institution, 1987.
Eberstadt, Nick. "Democracy and Development in East Asia." *National Affairs* (Fall 1989).
Economic Development Authority. *Updated Philippine Development Plan*. Manila: Government of the Philippines, 1984.
Fei, John C. H., Gustav Ranis, and Shirley W. Y. Kuo. *Growth With Equity: The Taiwan Case*. Washington: World Bank, 1979.
Galenson, Walter. *Economic Growth and Structural Change in Taiwan*. Ithaca: Cornell University Press, 1979.
Gee San. *A Critical Review of the Labor Standards Law in Taiwan*. Taipei: Ching-hua Institution for Economic Research, December, 1988.

———. *An Evaluation and International Comparison of Labor Laws and Regulations Which Affect Labor Costs in Taiwan.* Taipei: Chung-Hua Institution for Economic Research, 1989.

Heritage Foundation. *U.S. and Asia Statistical Handbook.* Washington, 1990.

Hongladarom, Chira, ed. *Comparative Labor and Management: Japan and Thailand.* Bangkok: Thamasart University Press, 1983.

International Labor Office. *Employment Issues and Policies for Thailand's Sixth Plan.* Geneva: I.L.O., 1985.

———. *Yearbook of Labor Statistics.* Geneva: I.L.O., various issues.

Kim, Jang Ho. *Wages, Employment and Income Distribution in South Korea.* New Delhi: ARTEP, 1985.

Kim, Kwang-suk, and Park Joon-kyung. *Sources of Economic Growth in Korea, 1963–1982.* Seoul: Korea Development Institute, 1985.

Kim, Taigi. *The Political Economy of Industrial Relations in Korea.* Seoul: Korea Labor Institute, 1989.

Korea (Republic of). *Yearbook of Labor Statistics.* Seoul, 1988.

Kuo, Shirley W. Y. "The Achievement of Growth with Equity." *Conference on Economic Development Experience of Taiwan.* Taipei: Institute of Economics, 1988.

Kuo, Shirley, and John C. H. Fei. "Causes and Roles of Export Expansion in the Republic of China." In *Foreign Trade and Investment,* edited by Walter Galenson. Madison: University of Wisconsin Press, 1985.

Lindauer, David. *Labor Market Behavior in the Republic of Korea.* Washington: World Bank, 1984.

Mabry, Bevars D. *The Development of Labor Institutions in Thailand.* Ithaca: Cornell University, Department of Asian Studies, 1979.

Mackie, J. A. C. "Economic Growth in the ASEAN Region." In *Achieving Industrialization in East Asia,* edited by Helen Hughes. Cambridge: Cambridge University Press, 1988.

Malaysia. *Fifth Malaysian Plan 1986–1990.* Kuala Lumpur, 1986.

———. *Survey of Manufacturing Industries.* Kuala Lumpur, various issues.

———. *Yearbook of Labor Statistics.* Kuala Lumpur, various issues.

Malonzo, Ibarra A. "Trade Unions as Participatory Agents in the Philippine Industrial Relations System." *Philippine Journal of Industrial Relations* nos 1–2 (1985).

Mitchell, Tony. *From a Developing to a Newly Industrialized Country: The Republic of Korea.* Geneva: I.L.O., 1988.

Montes, Manuel. "The Philippine Economy in the 1990s: Recovery and Restoration." In *Problems of Developing Countries in the 1990s,* vol. 2. Washington: World Bank, 1990.

Nash, Manning, ed. *Economic Performance in Malaysia.* New York: Paragon House, 1987.

Ofreno, Rene E., and Esther P. Habana. *The Employment Crisis and the World Bank's Adjustment Program*. Quezon: Institute of Industrial Relations, 1987.

Oshima, Harry. "Human Resources and Productivity Trends." In *Challenge of Asian Developing Countries*, edited by Shinichi Ichimura. Tokyo: Asia Productivity Organization, 1988.

Park, Se-il. "Labor Issues in Korea's Future." *World Development* 16, no. 1 (1988).

Philippines. Economic Development Authority. *Updated Philippine Development Plan, 1984–1987*. Manila, 1987.

————. *Yearbook of Labor Statistics*. Manila: various issues.

Richardson, Ray, and Byung Whan Kim. *Adjustments to Policy Changes: The Case of Korea, 1960–1985*. Washington: World Bank, 1986.

————. *The Structure of Labor Markets in LDCs: Overview of South Korea 1953–1984*. Washington: World Bank, 1986.

Sharma, Basu. *Basic Aspects of Industrial Relations in ASEAN*. Singapore: Institute of Southeast Asian Studies, 1985.

Siddiqui, A.M.A.H., ed. *Labor Administration Profile on Thailand*. Bangkok: International Labor Office, 1988.

Thailand. *Statistical Yearbook*. Bangkok: various issues.

Tidalgo, Rosa and Emmanuel F. Biguerra. *Philippine Employment in the 1970s*. Manila: Philippine Institute of Development Studies, 1982.

Tritasavit, Phiraphol. *Labor Policy and Practice in Thailand*. Ann Arbor, Michigan: University Microfilms, 1982.

U.S. Department of Labor. *Foreign Labor Trends: Korea*. Washington: GPO 1988–1989, 1989–1990.

————. *Foreign Labor Trends: Malaysia*. Washington: GPO 1987–1988, 1988–1989.

————. *Foreign Labor Trends: Philippines*. Washington: GPO 1987, 1988–1989, 1989–1990.

————. *Foreign Labor Trends: Taiwan*. Washington: GPO 1987, 1988–1989.

————. *Foreign Labor Trends: Thailand*. Washington: GPO 1990.

World Bank. *Korea: Managing the Industrial Transition*. Washington, 1987.

————. *Philippines: A Framework for Economic Recovery*. Washington, 1987.

————. *Social Indicators of Development*. Washington: various issues.

————. *Trends in Developing Economies*. Washington, 1990.

————. *World Development Report*. Washington, 1990.

————. *World Tables*. Washington, various issues.

Yeung, Irene. "Labor Gets Organized." *Free China Review*. October, 1990.

Index

ABOUT THE AUTHOR

WALTER GALENSON is Emeritus Professor of Economics at Cornell University. He was founder and first director of the Center for Chinese Studies at the University of California at Berkeley, founder of the World Employment Program of the International Labor Office in Geneva, and is a past-president of the Association for Comparative Economic Studies. Dr. Galenson is the author of 14 books, including most recently, *New Trends in Employment Practices: An International Survey* (Greenwood, 1991).